Operation: MIDDLE E
tary Mission to Reach Hollow Earth

Maps, and interior illustrations by the author.

Cover by Shawn Justin.

ISBN: 9798283017419

For information about permissions, rights, or bulk purchases, Spectorcreative.com

Printed in the United States of America
First Edition

123456789

Operation: MIDDLE EARTH
The Forgotten 1838 U.S. Military Mission to Reach Hollow Earth

By Scott D. Neitlich

Also, by the Author (*or coming soon!*):

INSTRUCTIONAL:

Doodling with Purpose: Hieroglyphs for the Modern Student

GRAPHIC NOVEL:

Myth Wars Vol 1: Zeus the Teenage Years

HISTORICAL NONFICTION: '

The Nile Quest: The Victorian Race to Uncover the Greatest Secret of the Ancient World

Columbus' Secret Mission: How Columbus hid his Jewish Heritage and his Quest for the Lost Tribes

The Dinosaur War: Revenge, Ruin, and the Race for the First Fossil Bones

Revenge of the Wolf: The Forgotten Admiral Who Shaped the Modern World

Fall of the West: The Epic Battle for Constantinople that Changed the World

Operation: MIDDLE EARTH. The Forgotten 1838 U.S. Military Mission to Reach Hollow Earth

The Time of Clive: The Battle that Shaped an Empire

VISUASLIZED CLASSICS:

Moby Dick by Herman Melville – *Visualized Edition*

Dedicated to Carl Bechtold and the McMahon for friendship and wonderful Thanksgiving conversations.

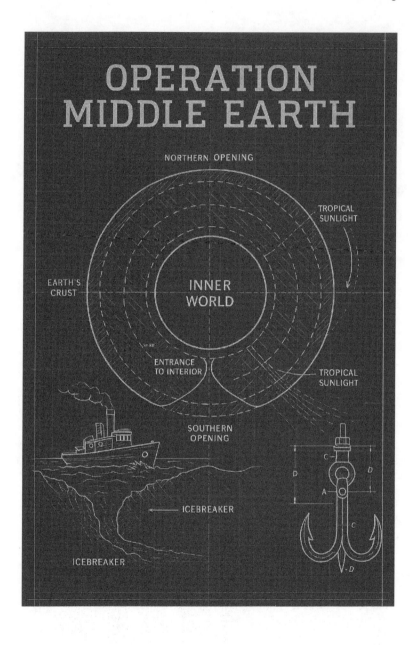

OPERATION MIDDLE EARTH

Forward:

Can you believe the United States military actually mounted an expedition to find a hole in the Earth?

Because it happened.

This isn't science fiction.

In 1838, the U.S. Navy launched what was, at the time, the most ambitious scientific and exploratory mission in American history: the U.S. Exploring Expedition. On the surface, it was about mapping coastlines and collecting botanical specimens.

But hidden beneath those official goals was something stranger—something inspired by a theory so audacious it straddled the line between genius and madness.

That theory? The Earth was hollow.

And someone believed it enough to risk ships, men, and lives to go find out.

The Hollow Earth idea has haunted us for centuries. From ancient myths of underworlds and lost cities to Enlightenment thinkers proposing concentric spheres beneath our feet, humanity has always looked down with a kind of reverent curiosity. What if *we're not standing on solid ground?* What if there's more—vast chambers, buried civilizations, or something older than time humming in the dark?

In the 1800s, it was an eccentric frontier obsession. By the 1930s, it had been twisted into fascist ideology. And in the internet age, it's become something else entirely—a digital legend that refuses to die. Scroll through YouTube, Reddit, TikTok, or Twitter, and you'll find it: satellite images with strange polar shadows, coordinates scrubbed from maps, leaked documents, whispery podcasts, memes, and spirals drawn in notebook margins by people who swear the Earth is hiding a secret.

And maybe it is.

This book is not a fantasy.

Everything in these pages—from the ship logs to the secret memos to the people who vanished without explanation—is rooted in real events. Where the record ends, we extrapolate. Where the facts are redacted, we descend into the spiral of what might be.

Because the Hollow Earth theory isn't just about geology.

It's about *possibility*.

It's about the dangerous thrill of asking "What if?" in a world where we've been told everything has already been discovered.

So come with us. Back to the edge of the map. Past the ice, beyond the silence, into the forgotten mission America never wanted to explain.

It's time to reopen the file.

It's time to look *down*.

-Scott Neitlich
Greensboro, NC 2025

USS Peacock

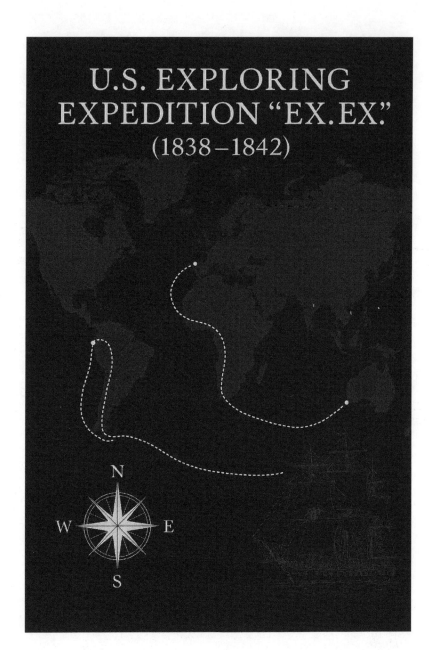

U.S. EXPLORING EXPEDITION "EX.EX."
(1838–1842)

"Final directive from Department of Naval Instruction:

Should an inner cavity or anomalous atmospheric breach be discovered, entry is at officer discretion under spiritual and national oath. No member of the press or public is to be made aware of this component of the mission until approved by presidential order."

— *Letter classified: REY-002-DARK*

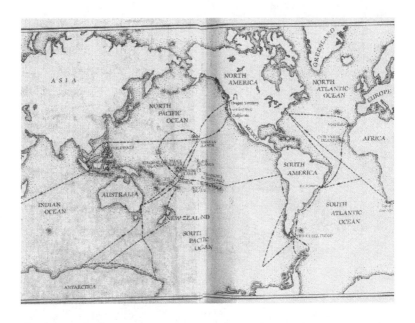

Introduction: Into the Spiral – A History of the Hollow Earth Theory

We have always looked down with wonder.

Before we looked to the stars, before we built cathedrals to the heavens or telescopes into the void, humanity turned its gaze toward the Earth beneath its feet. We dug graves, carved out homes, traced roots into the soil. The underworld—both feared and revered—was our first great mystery.

From the earliest myths to Enlightenment science, from ancient epics to internet conspiracies, the idea that something lies beneath the Earth's surface has refused to die. Some called it

Hell. Others, a paradise. A few, like John Cleves Symmes Jr., called it home.

This book is about the moment the United States took that idea seriously enough to send ships and men into the ice to find it.

Yes—this really happened.

But to understand why, we must begin much earlier.

I. Ancient Origins: The First Subterranean Myths

Long before Hollow Earth was a scientific theory, it was a sacred story.

In Mesopotamia, the Sumerians spoke of *Kur*, a land beneath the Earth guarded by demons and ruled by gods. The soul of the dead passed downward through seven gates, descending into shadow. The Greeks called it Hades. In Egypt, it was the

Duat, a realm Ra the sun god passed through each night, where the dead were judged and serpents circled the sky.

These weren't simply metaphors. For many ancient peoples, the underworld was as real as the stars—and sometimes more accessible. Volcanic craters, caves, and deep crevices were thought to be portals. When the earth trembled, it wasn't just tectonics—it was a voice, a stirring, a sign.

The Norse believed in Helheim, an icy domain below the roots of Yggdrasil, the World Tree. The Hebrew Sheol, the Hindu Patala, and the Buddhist Naraka all offered variations on the same truth: something lies beneath us.

Whether punishment, renewal, or mystery—it was there.
The spiral inward had begun.

II. Classical Curiosity: From Allegory to Anatomy

As myth gave way to philosophy, the nature of the Earth remained unresolved.
Plato hinted at lost realms beneath the Earth in his dialogues. In the *Phaedo*, he describes the Earth not as a flat plane or sphere, but as a "multifaceted, complex body with hollows, rivers, and great caverns," through which souls might travel.
Pythagoras envisioned a central fire within the Earth. So did Empedocles. These weren't hollow earths in the modern sense, but the idea of *layers*, *depth*, and even *interior life* had begun to take hold.

Then, in the 2nd century CE, Lucian of Samosata wrote *True History*, a satirical work often considered the first piece of science fiction. Among its bizarre contents: a trip inside the Earth.
By the time of the Roman Empire, the Earth's interior had become a theater for metaphysical debate, artistic metaphor, and emerging cosmology.

It would not stay theoretical for long.

III. The Medieval Descent: Spirals of Sin and Salvation

When Dante Alighieri wrote *Inferno* in the early 14th century, he mapped Hell as a literal structure within the Earth: nine concentric circles descending toward a frozen Lucifer at the core. Each circle held specific sinners, carefully categorized and poetically tormented.

But what's notable is not just the allegory—it's the *architecture*. Dante, like many medieval thinkers, believed the Earth was hollow—or at least partially so. Cathedrals were built to echo the cosmic order, and sermons described the Earth's interior not as molten rock, but as moral terrain.

This was the first time the spiral took shape as a narrative device: the deeper you went, the more truth you found—whether that truth was damnation or salvation.

Mystics and monks wrote of underground worlds inhabited by angels or devils. The Cathars of southern France whispered of an inner Earth paradise. Even the Templars, according to some accounts, believed in a hidden sanctuary beneath the Earth's crust.

But it would take the Enlightenment to turn belief into blueprint.

IV. Enlightenment Ambitions: Mapping the Impossible

In 1665, Jesuit scholar Athanasius Kircher published *Mundus Subterraneus*, a sprawling tome that included one of the first detailed diagrams of a Hollow Earth. His vision was not mystical, but mechanical: an Earth riddled with caverns, lava flows, underground oceans, and strange creatures.

It was part science, part art. And it caught fire.

Then came Edmond Halley.

In 1692, the astronomer famous for Halley's Comet proposed that the Earth consisted of nested concentric spheres—a hollow shell with smaller globes inside. He believed the inner spheres rotated separately and accounted for magnetic anomalies. Light from the core might even support life, he suggested.

Though his theory was eventually disproven, Halley's credentials gave it weight. Others followed. In 1741, the Norwegian theologian Ludvig Holberg wrote a Hollow Earth utopia, *Niels Klim's Underground Travels*. In 1781, the American clergyman Cotton Mather speculated that earthquakes were caused by "subterranean explosions" from hollow spaces.
The stage was set.

V. Symmes' Vision: From Eccentric to Expedition

In 1818, John Cleves Symmes Jr.—a former U.S. Army captain and merchant—sent a bold circular to governments, universities, and newspapers across America:

"I declare the Earth is hollow and habitable within; containing a number of solid concentric spheres, one within the other... I pledge my life in support of this truth and am ready to explore the inside of the Earth, if the world will support and aid me in the undertaking."

He requested 100 brave men and government funding to lead an expedition to the South Pole. His theory added a twist to Halley's: the Earth had vast holes at each pole, through which one could enter into the interior.

Symmes' ideas were mocked. Political cartoons showed him falling into a donut-shaped planet. Yet he was undeterred. He toured the country, giving lectures, building models, and slowly gathering supporters.
One of those was Jeremiah N. Reynolds—a writer, intellectual, and born orator.

Where Symmes was awkward and erratic, Reynolds was polished and persuasive. He rebranded Symmes' theory as a scientific endeavor and began lobbying Congress.
Incredibly, it worked.

In 1836, under growing public interest, Congress authorized the United States Exploring Expedition: six ships, hundreds of men, and a mandate to chart the South Seas and study natural phenomena.

But within its sealed orders was a second mission:
To investigate anomalies at the southern ice shelf.

VI. The Expedition That Vanished from Memory

The U.S. Exploring Expedition, or Ex. Ex., set sail in 1838 under Lieutenant Charles Wilkes. The official record describes cartography, natural history, and encounters with indigenous populations. But several journals and officer letters reference strange occurrences during the Antarctic phase.

Magnetic compasses malfunctioned. Wind patterns shifted erratically. One entry refers to "a strange warmth rising from beneath the ice." Another notes "a pressure in the head that worsens the deeper we go."

The expedition returned in 1842. Wilkes published his account. But many logs were redacted. Some specimens—marked with seals never explained—were delivered to a secure government office.

Reynolds, the expedition's greatest champion, vanished from the public eye. He died in obscurity.

Symmes had died earlier, in 1829. His grave in Hamilton, Ohio, bears a simple inscription: *He Contended That The Earth Is Hollow.*

The world moved on.

But the spiral had only deepened.

VII. From Science to Speculation

In 1864, Jules Verne published *Journey to the Center of the Earth*, blending Symmes' idea with volcanic access points and prehistoric life. In 1871, Edward Bulwer-Lytton introduced the world to *Vril*, an inner-Earth energy used by an advanced subterranean race.

These stories weren't treated as truth—but they weren't dismissed either.

In the 20th century, occult societies, Nazi mystics, and fringe explorers revived the Hollow Earth. Hitler reportedly funded expeditions to the South Pole and Tibet. The 1947 *Operation Highjump*—led by none other than Admiral Richard Byrd—ended abruptly, fueling decades of speculation.

Then came the internet.

Suddenly, Hollow Earth theory found new life. YouTube videos showed supposed satellite imagery of "holes" at the poles.

Reddit threads dissected seismic anomalies. TikToks invoked Byrd, Symmes, even Atlantis. The spiral had gone viral.

VIII. Why This Book

Operation Middle Earth is not about proving or disproving Hollow Earth theory.

It is about tracing the spiral—from Alexandria to Antarctica, from Symmes to Byrd, from myth to military operation. It is about the line where science blurs into belief, and belief into story.

Because belief matters.

Symmes believed enough to stake his life on it.

Reynolds believed enough to move Congress.

And somewhere, deep beneath the surface of the historical record, something still hums.

This book is written not to settle the debate, but to reopen the file.

To ask why the United States Navy once took Hollow Earth seriously.

To explore how myth shapes science—and how science sometimes walks straight into myth.

To document the expedition that tried to find the edge of the known world—and what may have found them instead.

Because the Earth, as it turns out, may not be hollow.

But our understanding of it still is.

And that is where the spiral begins.

Prologue: Into the Spiral – The Secret Flight of Admiral Byrd

Part I: The Sky Cracks Open

February 19, 1947
Arctic Circle – 0800 Hours

The Douglas R4D-5 Skytrain soared above an endless expanse of white. From horizon to horizon: nothing but wind-blasted flatness and the muted gleam of ice. Inside the cockpit, the rhythmic hum of the twin propellers was the only sound besides the occasional flip of a switch or the scratch of pen on paper. Rear Admiral Richard Evelyn Byrd sat straight-backed in the left-hand seat, eyes scanning the pale void ahead through frost-framed glass. His co-pilot, Lieutenant Hal Emery, leaned into the instruments, adjusting for minor drift.

"No change in wind," Hal muttered. "Holding altitude—twelve thousand feet. Outside temp minus forty-eight Fahrenheit."

Byrd nodded, jotting a brief note in his leather-bound flight log.

"We're due for the next waypoint in twenty minutes," Hal added, voice calm but edged with monotony. "I'm starting to think we're chasing ghosts."

"This whole region is a ghost," Byrd said, his voice low, reflective. "That's why we came. What better place to hide secrets?"

Hal gave a dry chuckle, then reached forward to tap the magnetic compass. It wavered, twitched once, then spun counterclockwise in a slow, sick spiral.

Byrd froze. "Did you see that?"

"Yeah." Hal tapped it again. Nothing changed. "Hold on."

Now the artificial horizon began to drift—listing unnaturally, as if the plane itself were rolling even though its flight path was perfectly level. Byrd instinctively adjusted the yoke, but there was no response from the plane.

"Instrumentation failure?" Byrd asked.

Hal's hands flew over switches. "I'm losing the altimeter—it's... climbing? No, wait—it's spinning. Jesus."

Byrd leaned over the console. The altimeter rotated in full revolutions, unmoored from any known altitude. Outside, the sky remained calm—no clouds, no storms, not even turbulence. Just that endless, pale nothing. But inside the cockpit, it felt as though the Earth had begun to come apart in fragments.

A low-frequency hum, just at the edge of hearing, began to vibrate through the fuselage. Not mechanical. Not natural.

"What the hell is that?" Hal's voice rose an octave.

"Radio," Byrd ordered.

Hal flicked the channel to shortwave. Static. He dialed to the emergency frequency—more static, followed by a brief pulse of something... rhythmic. A tone. Then silence.

"Magnetic interference?" Hal asked.

Byrd's hand went to the leather satchel at his side. From it, he retrieved the bulky handheld microphone of the flight recorder system. He thumbed the switch and began to dictate.

"Flight log—Entry 0817 hours. Instruments failing across the board. Compass non-functional. Altimeter and artificial horizon no longer aligned with aircraft behavior. Conditions outside remain visually normal, but anomalous readings suggest electromagnetic disruption. Requesting further analysis upon return."

He paused.

"Unusual vibration detected through hull. Audible hum—not mechanical."

As he spoke, the vibration ceased.

So did the hum.

The plane leveled on its own. The controls stiffened, then softened, then became responsive again. All at once, everything settled—as if a hand had smoothed a rippling cloth.

And the temperature began to rise.

First by one degree.

Then three.

Hal glanced at the thermometer. "Forty-two... Forty-one...

Thirty-nine..."

Byrd blinked. "That can't be."

"Something's wrong with the sensors."

"No," Byrd said. "Look at the windows."

Frost vanished like breath fading from a mirror. Outside, the white glare began to change—to darken—not to storm, but to color. Streaks of green and gray emerged beneath the snow, like the land itself was shifting its coat.

Then he saw it.

A break in the ice.

Not a crack—but a valley.

A long, plunging depression in the glacier, flanked by snow-capped ridges that curved in symmetrical arcs. Between them: no snow. No frost. No sign of the Arctic winter.

Instead—green.

Deep green.

Forests, rivers, and hills, thick with mist and motion.

Byrd gripped the yoke. "Altitude drop. Now."

Hal, pale and silent, obeyed. The Skytrain angled downward in a smooth glide. Byrd thumbed the recorder again.

"Flight log, 0823 hours. Impossible sighting confirmed. Coordinates unverified—somewhere beyond 86°N, estimated. Beneath the ice shelf: observed temperate biome—verdant, heavily forested valley between mountainous ridges. Initial impression suggests extensive geothermal activity or climatic anomaly."

He paused. Then spoke the words slowly.

"Temperature rising. Outside reading—thirty-one degrees Fahrenheit."

Hal was transfixed.

"Look..." he said, and pointed.

Byrd followed his gaze.

Near a winding river that cut between dark pines, a massive shape lumbered across the clearing. Covered in thick brown hair. Towering, trunked. The creature's silhouette moved with the sluggish weight of something prehistoric.

"Mammoth," Byrd whispered. "Christ... that looks like..."

The microphone dropped slightly in his hand and crackled loudly.

"... a mammoth."

Behind them, the plane's console flickered. Lights blinked out. Then back on. A dull red glow bathed the cockpit from below the dashboard.

The hum returned—but this time, higher-pitched.

Not from the hull.

From the sky.

No... from below.

Byrd turned off the recorder and reached instinctively for the window crank. It wouldn't move.

The Skytrain was descending—slowly, steadily—on its own.

"We're not flying this anymore," Hal said flatly.

Byrd's hands tightened around the yoke. "No. We're being flown."

They sat in stunned silence for several seconds as the aircraft continued its glide path toward the verdant world below.

Then—without warning—the radio sputtered.

A voice, filtered and oddly melodic, crackled through.

"You are safe. Do not be afraid."

Both men looked at each other in disbelief.

The voice repeated, clearer now.

"You are safe. Do not be afraid."

Byrd reached for the mic. "Identify yourself. This is a United States military aircraft. Identify your station."

No response.

Outside, shapes emerged from the cloud-bank.

Metallic, silent, and hovering.

Discs.

Two of them.

No rivets. No markings. Just smooth, seamless ovals glinting in the strange amber light now filtering from the horizon.

One moved alongside the left wing.

The other flanked the tail.

They kept pace without effort—no exhaust, no propulsion.

Just presence.

"Jesus Christ," Hal breathed. "What is this?"

Byrd's hand trembled as he wrote one final note in his log for the morning:

Escorted by unknown craft. Cannot confirm origin. Flight path no longer ours.

0831 Hours.

The Arctic is gone.

Something else has taken its place.

The valley widened below them.

At the far end, just beneath a line of jagged cliffs, a dark rift opened in the rock—a canyon that sloped downward like the throat of a great stone beast.

The plane banked gently to the right and angled toward it.

No controls moved.

No orders were given.

Byrd and Hal sat frozen, watching as the Skytrain dipped into the mouth of the earth.

Wordlessly, Hal reached forward and turned off the altimeter.

There was no need to know how deep they would go.

Not anymore.

They descended not into night, but into something brighter than the sky above.

The canyon opened gradually, the stone walls parting like the petals of a colossal, subterranean flower. Byrd's Skytrain passed silently between them, no turbulence, no drag—only that humming, harmonic vibration pulsing gently through the airframe.

Hal whispered, "It's like flying through a throat."

The walls of the gorge were slick with moisture, veined with quartz and faintly luminous minerals. Greens and golds shimmered along the surfaces, as if the very rock were lit from within. Mist curled in slow spirals across the widening passage, and far below, the black glass of a river snaked through the valley floor.

Ahead, the tunnel mouth yawned wide—an impossible structure, smooth and symmetrical, like an engineered arch cut clean into the mountain. No light escaped from it. The plane entered that opening like a bird flying into the pupil of an eye.

They passed into the dark.

Then, light.

Every surface within the chamber—ceiling, walls, floor—radiated soft luminescence. Not from a central source, but from the material itself. It glowed like frost kissed by starlight. The Skytrain leveled out, no longer descending, but gliding forward down a vast crystalline corridor that arced gently with the curve of the Earth—or what Byrd assumed was still Earth.
Except... the world outside no longer looked like anything terrestrial.

The canyon had opened into a massive cavernous realm—a dome so high it defied comprehension. Mountains jutted from beneath an amber sky. Trees—actual trees, not stalagmites—rose hundreds of feet tall, their trunks translucent, their leaves glowing faintly green and blue. Waterfalls flowed not just downward but sideways, bending across rock walls as if pulled by some unseen gravity well.

Below them, the river split and twisted into a delta that fed into lakes of clear sapphire. Across one of the lakebeds, massive creatures grazed—some with sweeping horns, others with crests like dragons in a medieval tapestry. One spread leathery wings and launched into the air, banking across their path before soaring into the heights of the chamber dome.

"Pterosaurs," Byrd muttered. "That's a... that's a goddamn pterosaur."

Hal had stopped speaking. He stared out the window, lips parted, as if unable to process the scene before them.

The radio crackled again.

"This is Arianni escort. Your path is safe. We are taking you to First Threshold. Remain calm."

Byrd resisted the urge to respond.

"Do we follow them?" Hal asked.

"We're not flying anymore," Byrd said flatly. "We're guests. Or prisoners. Depending on the next five minutes."

The saucers flanking their wings glided slightly ahead, leading them down the valley. Beneath, what appeared to be roadways and aqueducts spiderwebbed across the land—constructed, orderly, but with curves and arcs that seemed more grown than built. Occasionally, spires jutted from the landscape—organic, crystalline, and many stories tall, their sides etched with patterns that shimmered as they passed.

The plane suddenly tilted—slightly, but firmly. A new descent began, slow and smooth, as if carried by invisible cables.

Ahead, the land dropped into a basin ringed by obsidian cliffs.

At its center stood a vast cavern mouth—circular, massive, and perfectly symmetrical. Along its rim were glowing runes or glyphs, etched in a pattern that suggested both mathematics and language.

The Skytrain dipped toward this new aperture.

"We're going in," Hal whispered. His knuckles were white against the armrest.

Byrd opened the recorder again.

"Flight Log—0855 Hours. No longer in Arctic airspace. Descended into inner basin structure. Surrounded by biome inconsistent with any known polar terrain. Flora and fauna predate Holocene epoch. Escort craft continue to direct our trajectory. Unknown energy source appears to govern gravitational effect on aircraft."

He paused, staring down at the mouth of the Earth.

"This is no longer the Arctic. This is something else entirely."

As they entered the cavern, a sensation passed over both men—not of motion, but of transition. The light changed—softer, whiter, more diffused. Ahead, the air shimmered like heat mirage. Then, they were inside.

The space beyond the basin defied classification.

It was not a cave.

It was not a tunnel.

It was a world.

A vast interior horizon stretched out before them—mountains, forests, rivers, all lit by a soft, omnipresent glow that had no source and cast no shadows. Above, the sky curved upward—not into blackness, but into more land. An inverted landscape mirrored the one below them, as if they were flying through the inner surface of a hollow globe.

Byrd gasped.

"So it's true... it's all true."

He had read the Symmes theory in passing. Dismissed it, mostly. Hollow Earth ideas belonged to fringe science, crackpot dreamers. But this—this wasn't theory. This wasn't conjecture.

This was terrain.

This was inhabited.

Shapes moved along ridgelines. Dots of light traced through the sky—craft like their escorts, darting without trails or sound.

Towers the size of skyscrapers jutted up (or down?) from the horizon. Domes, too—clear, crystalline, humming with a resonance that vibrated in Byrd's ribs.

He opened the log again.

"0901 Hours. We are inside what appears to be a vast spherical cavity. Inner surface supports full biome, infrastructure, and possibly cities. Atmospheric conditions consistent with temperate zone—estimated 70°F. Gravity holding stable. No evidence of centrifugal effect."

The plane tilted again. Ahead, one of the crystalline domes enlarged rapidly—a great transparent canopy beneath which structures of silver and blue rose in elegant arcs. The saucers guiding them peeled away.

The Skytrain angled down... and began to land.

The wheels touched down without a jolt. The runway glowed faint blue beneath the aircraft as if absorbing kinetic energy.

The brakes did not engage, but the plane came to a stop.

No engines. No power. No human guidance.

They had arrived.

Silence.

Hal finally unbuckled. "Should we... step out?"

Before Byrd could answer, the plane door clicked. Not loudly, but with certainty. Then it began to open.

Byrd took a breath and reached for his sidearm.

Hal looked at him.

"I don't think that'll help here, Admiral."

Byrd nodded and let it go.

They stepped onto the glowing tarmac.

The air was fresh. Not sterile, not artificial—just... perfect. No scent of ozone or metal. Just faint earth and pine, the way a forest smells at sunrise.

A party awaited them—five figures, tall and robed in white and blue garments. They had the appearance of humans but were taller, more symmetrical. Their skin was pale, almost translucent, and their eyes shone like polished silver. No weapons. No posturing. Just presence.

One stepped forward and spoke—not aloud, but into their minds.

"Welcome, Admiral Richard Byrd. Welcome, Lieutenant Emery. You are safe. You have entered Arianni, First Threshold of the Inner World."

Byrd's jaw tightened. "You know who we are."

"We have known of your approach for some time."

"How?"

"We watched."

Another figure gestured toward a transport—an elegant craft hovering silently a few inches from the ground. Like a gondola with no rails, no supports, yet glowing softly from beneath. A ramp extended.

Byrd looked at Hal.

"You okay?"

Hal nodded. "Are you?"

"No."

They stepped aboard.

The transport lifted and began to glide toward the central dome—its surface iridescent like mother-of-pearl. Below, gardens unfolded—terraced and floral, with colors Byrd could not name. The path curved gently until a massive structure came into view, its spires twisting like vines and topped with floating crystal orbs.

The transport slowed.

Another voice entered their minds—this one deeper, older.

"You have passed the threshold. Few ever do. Fewer return.

But return you shall. With a message."

Byrd sat forward. "Who are you?"

"We are of the Inner World. And it is time you understood what that means."

Part II: The City Beneath the World

The transport halted soundlessly before a grand archway carved from crystal and stone. The surface shimmered with moving light—ripples like heat waves dancing across etched symbols that glowed softly as Byrd and Hal approached. The air inside the chamber was impossibly pure. Cool but not cold.

Vibrant, not sterile. Every breath felt like the first after a long illness.

Byrd hesitated before stepping through the threshold. There was no door, no hinge—just an opening. As he passed through, the arch flared with soft light, then dimmed.

The interior was vast.

A hall, cathedral in scale but alien in design. Massive pillars of translucent quartz spiraled upward like growing vines, supporting a vaulted ceiling covered in tessellated patterns that shifted color as one walked beneath them. The floor was smooth stone veined with glowing lines—perhaps energy conduits or symbolic maps. At the far end, an open portal led to a platform overlooking the jungle below.

This was no cave.

It was a city.

And it was alive.

As Byrd and Hal advanced, they were flanked on either side by their escorts—tall, robed beings with eyes that shimmered in the ambient light. They communicated wordlessly, guiding the two men through a series of corridors lined with bas-reliefs—

scenes of harvest, astronomy, oceans rising and falling, and strange devices that looked both ancient and advanced.

Hal slowed beside one of the murals. "This one… this is a solar system. That's Earth. But there's a twelfth body."

Byrd stopped too. "A hidden planet?"

"Or a forgotten one."

They were urged onward.

The corridor opened into another chamber—smaller, circular, and humming with low vibration. A clear platform hovered over what appeared to be a vast map—three-dimensional, shifting like water. Landmasses appeared and disappeared. Volcanoes bloomed. Cities flickered into being, then vanished under waves.

"We call this the Orb of Memory," said a voice behind them.

They turned. A new figure entered—shorter than the others, cloaked in green, and hooded. His face was partially visible:

aged, not frail, with skin like polished ivory and eyes like storm clouds.

"I am the Keeper of Thresholds," he said aloud. His voice echoed in the room but also resonated in Byrd's chest. "I am to escort you to the Central Dome. You will meet the Arianni Council there. And then—if you are ready—the Master."

Byrd and Hal followed him in silence.

They entered another transport, this one faster. It glided along a translucent rail through an underground jungle glowing with bio-luminescent flora. Trees spiraled like cathedral spires. Vines pulsed with light. Insects—if that's what they were—buzzed with radiant wings, and reptilian creatures slithered through water that sparkled as if laced with stars.

"Is this natural?" Hal asked quietly.

"It is guided," the Keeper replied. "All nature is, to some degree."

Far in the distance, a beam of light pulsed from the earth into the sky—an axis mundi piercing the dome's zenith. They were heading toward it.

Byrd leaned closer to the window, watching a herd of what could only be described as antlered elephants grazing beneath glowing trees. Two juveniles splashed in a crystalline river while a larger bull trumpeted at something unseen.

The Keeper observed their amazement. "You are not the first to see this place. But you are among the very few who may speak of it."

"May?" Byrd asked. "Or will?"

"That depends on what you choose to hear."

The transport entered a tunnel of soft amber light, and emerged in the shadow of a massive dome—larger than any Byrd had seen on the surface. It resembled a pearl set into the earth, reflecting both jungle and starlight.

At the entrance stood a delegation of figures—some Arianni, others clearly not. One had the features of an ancient Asian noble. Another resembled a Native elder wrapped in turquoise and feathered fabric. One looked impossibly similar to a medieval European monk.

Byrd stared.

The Keeper nodded. "The surface has always been watched.

And helped. These are the Stewards."

The group bowed as Byrd and Hal disembarked. No words were spoken, but Byrd felt a resonance move through his body, like a bell tolling just beneath the range of hearing.

They entered the dome.

Inside, the ceiling arced far overhead—so high it was barely visible—and pulsed with a soft, cloudlike glow. Floating platforms hovered in the open space, and transparent walkways spanned massive vertical gardens. Light flowed through the structure like wind. Water shimmered in hanging canals. Everything felt grown, not built.

"This is the Central Dome," the Keeper said. "All inner-world activity moves through here—science, energy, thought. We do not separate disciplines as you do above."

Byrd took it in, overwhelmed

"How long has this been here?"

"Arianni predates the surface you know," said the Keeper. "Long before Babel. Long before the Deluge."

"Atlantis?" Hal muttered.

The Keeper smiled. "That was one of our children."

A lift descended—no cables, no buttons, just a soft pulse of blue light. They stepped inside. The lift moved upward without inertia, friction, or sound.

At the summit, they entered a crystalline chamber lined with curved panels, each showing images of Earth—mountains, oceans, cities, skies, all in real time.

One showed Washington, D.C.

Another, Hiroshima—still recovering from scars less than two years old.

Another, the Amazon, already beginning to smolder.

"This is the Mirror Ring," the Keeper said. "We observe your world not to control it, but to understand it—and to prepare for when it might need help. Or... when it becomes a threat."

Byrd stared at the panels. "You think we're dangerous."

"We know you are," the Keeper said.

The far wall slid open.

They entered a final chamber—silent, circular, empty but for a single dais at the center. On it: two chairs, and one curved structure that looked like a speaking shell, humming faintly.

The Keeper gestured.

"Sit. The Master comes."

Byrd sat slowly. Hal stood behind him, arms crossed tightly.

The light dimmed.

Then a form emerged—not walked, not floated, but unfolded—from the shadows. A being taller than the others.

Wreathed in energy. Clothed in shifting robes that changed hue as it moved. Its face was both young and impossibly old. Its eyes contained galaxies.

It sat.

The chamber quieted.

A voice—not from the mouth, but from everywhere—spoke:

"You have come far, Admiral Byrd. Farther than most. And now you must know: You are in Arianni. We are of the Inner World. And we have been waiting."

Byrd swallowed. "Waiting for what?"

"For the moment when your people would reach the threshold. When your weapons could shatter worlds. When your skies could burn. When your faith in power outpaced your faith in each other."

Hal spoke, his voice cracking. "Why us?"

"Because you still listen. And because you still might turn back."

Byrd looked up at the Master. "Are you gods?"

"No. We are your cousins. Your mirror. We once walked among you. Then you chose conquest. So we withdrew. But the spiral turns. And it brings us here again."

Silence fell.

Then Byrd asked the only question that mattered.

"What do you want us to do?"

The Master regarded Byrd in silence, though silence here was never empty.

Energy pulsed gently through the chamber—faint concentric waves radiating from the dais. Byrd felt it in his bones, like the distant toll of a bell underwater. It did not hurt. But it demanded attention.

"You ask what we want you to do," the Master said. "But first you must know what has already been done."

Byrd leaned forward. "I'm listening."

"Your people have reached the second great threshold. The first was fire. The second is the atom. The third, you are not ready for."

Hal, still standing, shifted. "What is the third?"

"Consciousness. The unification of will and energy. What you call spirit. What your ancestors once knew before they chose dominion over harmony."

The chamber dimmed.

A panel behind the Master brightened to reveal Earth—blue and turning slowly in the void.

It zoomed closer, faster, until images began to flash in rapid succession: mushroom clouds rising above atolls and deserts.

Forests burning. Cities flooding. Skies choked with smoke. Animals dying in silence.

Then came other images.

Faces.

Children.

Men in uniform. Women in prayer. The old and the forgotten.

All staring upward. All asking the same silent question: *Why?*

Byrd looked away.

"We are not all like this," he said. "Many of us want peace."

The Master nodded.

"That is why you were chosen. You, who explored not for conquest but for understanding. But good men cannot prevent calamity if they remain silent."

Hal stepped forward. "What do you expect us to do? Go back and tell them we found paradise inside the Earth? No one will believe us."

"They will not. At first."

Another image appeared.

A man standing before a crowd, holding a scroll. His face was obscured, but his presence radiated strength. Around him: chaos. Behind him: fire.

"But the seed must be planted."

Byrd looked at the Master. "Why now?"

"Because you are standing at the edge. One more step and the fall is irreversible. Your weapons are capable of unmaking the planet. Your leaders are not yet aware of what lies beyond victory—desolation."

He rose—not standing, but ascending, robes billowing though there was no wind.

"You must carry this message. Tell your world: there is another path. Tell them we still watch. And that they were not abandoned. Only given time."

A new image bloomed around them—not on a screen, but in the very air. A three-dimensional vision, wrapping them in light and memory.

Byrd saw a vast plain, long before cities.

He saw luminous beings walking among early humans—teaching, healing, guiding.

He saw temples rise not to gods, but to unity.

Then the wars came.

Spears turned to blades. Blades to bullets. Bullets to bombs.

And the luminous ones withdrew, one by one, until the world forgot they were ever real.

"We withdrew. But we did not vanish," the Master said.

Byrd stood slowly, heart pounding.

"Why me? Why now?"

The Master's voice became almost... human.

"Because you came looking."

Silence filled the chamber once more.

Then the Master turned to Hal. "You are afraid."

Hal didn't deny it. "Yes."

"Do not be ashamed. It is good to be afraid before the truth."

Byrd stepped forward. "And if we speak of this—if we tell the world—what happens?"

"Most will laugh. Some will listen. A few will try to bury it. But time will unearth what fear tries to hide. Speak anyway."

Hal lowered his head. "I can't do this."

The Master looked at him. Not with judgment, but with deep understanding.

"Then be still. The message is not for everyone. Not all seeds take root."

Byrd touched Hal's shoulder, gently guiding him back. "I'll carry it."

The Master extended a hand.

In it appeared a glowing object—smooth, palm-sized, and warm with an inner light.

Byrd accepted it.

"It will guide you if you let it. And it will remain hidden if you are not ready."

The object pulsed once in his hand, then dimmed. He slipped it into his pocket without thinking. It felt like memory.

"You're letting us go?" Byrd asked.

"We never held you. You held yourselves."

The chamber began to brighten.

The dais lowered. A new escort approached—silent, calm, waiting.

"You will return to your plane. It has been made whole. Your records remain. Though some will not remember all that occurred."

Hal looked up, suddenly startled. "Wait—what do you mean—"

He swayed.

Then collapsed.

Byrd rushed to him. "Hal!"

He was breathing, but his eyes stared past Byrd into something far away. Tears streamed silently down his cheeks.

The Master looked down at him.

"He has seen too much. His soul recoils, but he will heal. When he is ready, he will remember."

Byrd stood slowly. "Will I forget too?"

"Not unless you wish it."

"No," Byrd said. "I'll remember."

"Then be ready. For your world will not."

They were led back through the Central Dome. This time, everything was quieter. The glowing plants dimmed as they passed. The paths were empty. The light softened.

The Skytrain waited on the tarmac as if it had never left.

Byrd helped Hal into the cockpit. He stared straight ahead, silent.

"Will he fly?"

"The plane will."

Byrd nodded.

He climbed in. The hatch sealed behind them. The controls lit up—familiar, tangible, comforting.

The humming began again, and the plane lifted without engine.

As it rose, Byrd looked out the side window one last time.

The Master stood on the platform, hands raised—not in farewell, but in reminder.

Then the dome receded.

The tunnel narrowed.

The light dimmed.

And they rose.

The ascent was longer than the descent—time dilated strangely, as if each moment stretched to examine him, test him, ask if he would forget what he saw.

He did not.

The Skytrain emerged from the canyon mouth in silence. The Arctic sun gleamed in the distance, and white once again ruled the horizon.

The plane drifted above the ice, engines now sputtering back to life.

Hal stirred.

"Are we... back?"

Byrd looked at the instruments.

Altitude: 10,200 feet.

Latitude: unknown.

Compass: stable.

He didn't answer.

The radio crackled.

"Bravo Station to Skytrain—do you copy?"

Byrd pressed the mic. "Copy, Bravo. Skytrain reporting. Two crew aboard. Request position fix."

There was a long silence.

"Skytrain, you disappeared from radar four hours ago. We were preparing a search grid. What is your last known position?" Byrd looked at Hal.

"I'll send coordinates shortly. Please advise on nearest recovery ship."

As the transmission continued, he opened the flight log and added a final line.

February 19, 1947 – 1630 Hours
Aircraft returned. Crew intact. Memories... uncertain.

They said I must speak.

And so I will.

Part III: Silence and Shadow

The wind howled again.

Real wind, cold and sharp, not the whispering stillness of the Hollow Earth. Byrd tightened his flight jacket and stepped onto the icy tarmac of the USS *Mount Olympus*, a U.S. Navy recovery vessel positioned several hundred miles north of where they'd last been seen on radar.

The Skytrain had touched down on the frozen ice sheet without incident. The engines worked. The gauges read normally.

Hal had come out of his catatonia sometime during the final hour of the return flight but remembered almost nothing. He blinked, answered questions, and performed basic flight protocol—but when Byrd said the words "Arianni" or "Inner World," Hal's face went blank.

No recognition. No protest.

Just… absence.

The deck officer approached briskly, saluting.

"Admiral Byrd. Lieutenant Emery. Orders are to bring you both below deck for medical evaluation and debriefing immediately."

Byrd returned the salute without speaking.

They were escorted into the belly of the ship. Everything felt too bright. Too loud. The clanging of boots on steel. The electric hum of overhead lights. It grated against the memory of the crystalline silence he had just left behind.

They were split up at once.

Hal was taken to the infirmary. Byrd was shown into a small, windowless room. A cot. A steel desk. One chair. One light.

And a guard outside the door.

He waited.

No clock on the wall.

No sense of how long had passed.
Eventually, a man in a white lab coat entered with a clipboard and a neutral expression.

"Admiral, we're going to take your vitals and run a basic neurological screen. Standard procedure following unscheduled Arctic flight loss."

Byrd complied. He was poked, measured, scanned. Blood drawn. Reflexes tested. Questions asked. He answered automatically, giving only what was verifiable.

Where did you take off?

What was your last known heading?

When did your radio stop working?

No one asked the right questions.

Or maybe they didn't want to.

That night, he was allowed to sleep.

At 0400 hours, the door opened again.

This time, three men entered. One wore a Navy uniform. One wore Air Force insignia. The third wore a dark gray suit with no markings. Civilian. Older. Clean-shaven. Eyes like iron filings.

"Admiral Byrd," the man in the suit said. "We've read your preliminary flight log."

Byrd didn't move.

"You're going to tell us everything. Off the record."

"I've already submitted my logs," Byrd said.

"No," the civilian said quietly. "We want what's *not* in them."

The Navy officer interjected. "We tracked your plane's return—radar shows you re-entered from a trajectory impossible to achieve in your fuel window. Your transponder showed you traveling *northwest* of your original flight plan. That would put you... somewhere beyond the polar cap."

Byrd remained silent.

"Admiral," the Air Force officer said, "you were off the grid for nearly four hours. That's not a mechanical failure. That's a vanishing."

Byrd studied them.

"You tell me what you think happened," he said evenly.
The civilian leaned forward, hands clasped.

"There are rumors," he said. "Russian expeditions disappearing. German flights during the war that never came back. Old Norse myths about warm lands beyond the snow. And now you—highly decorated, highly credible—return with a plane that landed itself, a flight path no one can trace, and a co-pilot who looks like he's seen God and forgotten the face."
He paused.

"We don't want to hurt you. But we will contain this."

Byrd met his eyes. "You mean suppress."

"If necessary."

The civilian stood.

"You are under temporary classified directive. Everything you saw, recorded, or imagined beyond checkpoint Bravo is now a matter of national security."
Byrd's face darkened. "I won't lie."

"We're not asking you to lie," the civilian said. "We're asking you to *forget*."

The officers left without waiting for a reply.

Later that day, his logs were taken.

The entire flight record—including backup tapes—was boxed, tagged, and carried away by personnel Byrd didn't recognize.

Even the dictation recorder in the cockpit was removed.

He asked to speak with Hal. He was told Hal was undergoing "further medical review" and was "not fit for conversation."

Byrd knew what that meant.

They were isolating them.

Compartmentalizing them.

Byrd began writing.
With pen and paper—what they hadn't yet confiscated. He scribbled pages of memory, diagrammed the city of Arianni from every angle he could recall, wrote down what the Master had said. He didn't know how long he had until they took this, too.

When the paper ran out, he etched symbols into the underside of his cot using a broken coat hanger.

The ship docked in Reykjavik under radio silence.

He was flown to Andrews Air Force Base in Maryland within the day.

Washington was gray, overcast, and full of locked doors.

He met again with the civilian and three new men in darker suits.

They gave him coffee. A seat. A warning.

"You are being awarded a citation for meritorious Arctic flight conduct under Operation Highjump," the civilian said. "It will come with press. But only the press we allow."

Byrd sipped the coffee.

"This wasn't part of Highjump."

"No," the man said. "It wasn't. Which is why it never happened."

They handed him a nondisclosure document. Top Secret. Violation punishable by court-martial and, if deemed espionage, potential execution under the Espionage Act.
"You will say nothing," the man said. "Not about caverns. Not about creatures. Not about Arianni. And especially not about being contacted."

Byrd raised an eyebrow. "So you know."

The man didn't answer.

"Then why the charade?"

"Because people like stories," the civilian said. "They don't like truth. Especially when it threatens to undo everything they think they know."

Byrd signed.

He had no choice.

His diary was redacted.

The pages he'd written disappeared. His personal copy of the logbook was returned with full sections blacked out—whole entries removed, references to temperature anomalies, the mammoth, the guiding aircraft—all excised.

He was promoted.

Ceremonially.

Given a new flight mission to South America—a goodwill tour, meaningless in scope but high in visibility.

They sent Hal to a VA hospital in Connecticut. Official diagnosis: exhaustion. Byrd was not permitted to contact him.

No newspapers mentioned the delay in Arctic communications.
No reports questioned the irregularity of the Skytrain's return path.

And just like that, the Arctic sealed its mouth.

And the world moved on.

Washington, D.C.
April 3, 1947

Admiral Byrd stood alone in the dim hallway of the Hay-Adams Hotel, staring at the door to Room 608. Behind it, the world outside throbbed with the indifferent pulse of government. Men in suits hurried to meetings. Cars rattled over cobblestones. Radios blared news of the latest hearings on Capitol Hill. The war was over. The Cold War had begun. No one wanted to talk about warm jungles under the ice.

He turned the key and entered.

The room was modest, with floral curtains and a small writing desk. A fruit bowl had been delivered by the concierge. He didn't touch it.

Instead, he locked the door behind him and pulled the desk chair tight to the table. From the inner pocket of his uniform coat, he withdrew a small black journal—new, leather-bound, unopened.

He set it on the desk.

The television in the corner buzzed softly, flickering a black-and-white image of a senator giving a speech about steel subsidies.

Byrd turned it off.

He picked up a fountain pen and opened the journal.
His hand trembled slightly as he pressed the nib to the first page.

Then stopped.

What could he say?

What could he *ever* say?

They had taken everything else—his voice, his reports, his records, his co-pilot. They had returned him to the world only after first ensuring that he no longer belonged in it. He was a man split in two—one half walking in the public light, the other trapped in a hidden chamber of ice and memory.

Still, the message had to be preserved.

Even if unread. Even if unseen.

Someone, someday, would find it.

He began to write.

There is another world.

And it is beautiful.

And we were not ready for it.

He paused.

Outside, a siren wailed in the street. Somewhere, a newspaper vendor called the evening headlines. Congress had voted to increase atomic research funding.
Byrd closed his eyes.
He saw the glowing trees again. The beasts with ancient eyes.

The Master's final gaze.

He saw Hal's vacant stare, the tears that had fallen without reason or memory.

He saw the great crystal dome rising in silence from the valley floor.

He kept writing.

They live beneath us—not in tunnels or fables, but in a space forgotten by time. They are not monsters. They are not invaders. They are not gods. They are watchers.

Their message was simple: change, or perish.

He turned the page.

I was told to speak. I was told to share what I saw. But they—the ones above ground—have decided otherwise. They fear what cannot be controlled. What cannot be monetized.

They fear the idea that Earth still holds secrets. That we are not alone. That there is more to our history than we are permitted to remember.

He flipped to the back of the journal and sketched what he remembered of the Arianni emblem—a spiral within a circle, surrounded by radiating lines. A symbol of wholeness. Of paths not yet taken.

He closed the journal and placed it beneath the floorboard beneath the dresser. A loose plank, unnoticed. He covered it with the hotel's welcome mat.

If they came for him again, they would not find this.
Not this time.

Two weeks later

Naval Command, Washington Navy Yard

Byrd stood before a row of high-ranking officials in a narrow briefing room. The walls were bare. The windows blacked out.

Four flags flanked the dais—U.S. Navy, Department of Defense, Joint Chiefs, and Presidential Seal.

He was not invited to sit.

A two-star admiral stepped forward and cleared his throat.

"Rear Admiral Byrd, thank you for your report on Operation Highjump. Your findings have been evaluated, reviewed, and

deemed satisfactory in all classified respects. You are instructed not to discuss details outside the confines of this room. Do you understand?"

"I do."

"You are hereby reassigned to ceremonial diplomatic service.

Your next assignment will be an extended goodwill tour of South America. You will speak at military academies, consulates, and cultural forums. You will represent American aviation excellence and global cooperation."

Byrd didn't respond.

"Your itinerary will be transmitted directly to your aide. Any questions?"
He raised a hand.

"Yes?"

"Will I be permitted to contact my co-pilot?"

A beat of silence.

Then: "Lieutenant Emery has been medically retired under section 9-B. He is not permitted contact. For his safety."

Byrd's face darkened.

"For *his* safety."

"Yes, Admiral. Dismissed."

Byrd turned and walked out without saluting.

Buenos Aires, Argentina
May 22, 1947

The ballroom shimmered with light and champagne.

He stood in dress whites, shaking hands with ambassadors, local officials, and eager cadets. The band played Glenn Miller.

Photographers flashed bulbs. The room pulsed with forced optimism.

No one asked about the ice.

No one asked about the light that came from stone or the beings who never aged.

No one asked about Arianni.
He smiled, nodded, delivered his speech about polar aviation and the courage of American explorers.

Then he retired to his hotel.

Room 407.

He removed a new journal from his case.
Opened it.

Wrote only one line:

The spiral still turns.

Then he turned out the lights.

What Byrd never knew was that he was not the first.

Another mission had come before him—a U.S. Navy squad dispatched under orders sealed by Congress and buried in silence.

Their mission was official.

Their story was forgotten.

Until now.

End of Prologue

John Symmes Jr

Chapter 1: Symmes' Hole – The Man Who Declared Earth Hollow

The wind came in cold off the river, the kind that rustles banners and dust in equal measure. On the edge of St. Louis, beneath a heavy April sky in 1818, a thin man climbed onto a wooden crate and declared war on the known world. His coat was threadbare, his voice unshakable. In one hand, he held a wooden globe he'd carved himself, split at both poles. In the other, he held a stack of papers, still damp from the press.

"To all the world," he cried, "I declare the Earth is hollow and habitable within!"

Some in the crowd laughed. Some muttered and walked on. But a few—perhaps more than he expected—stood frozen.

The man's name was John Cleves Symmes Jr. And that morning, he did something no American had ever done: he staked his life, reputation, and future on the idea that beneath our feet, beneath the crust and the stone, lay another world. And that he—Symmes—was the man destined to find it.

He had no funding. No expedition. No scientific society backing his claim. What he had was a theory he couldn't shake. One that had crept into his dreams, seized his waking hours, and refused to let go.

He had served in the War of 1812, a captain of artillery, stationed at the northern forts. He'd fought and survived. After the war, like many veterans, he pushed west, opened a trading post, and tried to carve a life out of the Ohio frontier. He failed. The land beat him. The market turned against him. His debts mounted. But in that wilderness, something else had taken root.

He had read Edmond Halley's theories from the previous century—the ones dismissed as fanciful by European science.

Halley, the same man who tracked the comet that bears his name, had proposed that the Earth might be hollow: not a single shell, but multiple concentric spheres. A luminous inner sun. A subterranean world. At the time, it was speculation—idle musings of a genius who stared too long at the stars.

Edmond Halley

Symmes saw something more.

He discarded the nested shells. Simplified the design. No inner sun. Just a massive cavity, with vast polar openings—thousands of miles across. Airy, habitable, temperate. A place where rivers flowed, birds migrated, and unknown civilizations might still thrive.

He believed it with a faith that could only come from fire.

He printed five hundred copies of his first circular and mailed them out at his own expense—to every university, library, scientific journal, and government office he could find. Each was hand-signed. Each carried the same message: not just that the Earth was hollow, but that he was willing to prove it.

Willing to lead an expedition to the poles. Willing to risk everything.

He waited for a response.

What came first was silence.

Then laughter.

The press had a field day. Cartoons depicted Symmes standing on a globe like a peeled orange, ships sailing into gaping holes at the poles. Satirical poems rhymed "Symmes" with "whims." He became a walking punchline. And yet, he didn't stop.

He took to the road with a wooden globe and a set of lecture notes. From town to town he went—Cincinnati, Pittsburgh, Lexington—speaking to whoever would listen. His words were strange but magnetic. There was something about his conviction that made it hard to dismiss him entirely.

Some threw rotten vegetables.

Some listened until the end.

A few asked questions.

And a very small number began to believe.

They called themselves Symmesites. Not kooks, but lawyers, businessmen, clergy. Men who believed that the Earth was not fully known—that there were secrets the textbooks hadn't yet printed. That maybe, just maybe, this broken ex-soldier from Ohio had stumbled onto something real.

One of them was James McBride, a respected Ohio land surveyor and amateur scientist. He joined the cause, published a defense of the theory, and began petitioning Congress for an official expedition. And somehow, impossibly, the idea found its way to the floor of the House of Representatives.

In 1823, a formal request was introduced for federal funds to mount a polar expedition under Captain Symmes' command.

The proposal didn't pass. But it made the record. Somewhere, in the archives of the young American republic, a document exists showing that the government once considered sending men to the edge of the world to look for a hole.

And at the time, sitting in the White House, was President John Quincy Adams.

Adams never spoke publicly on Symmes. But he had a deep respect for scientific inquiry and the uncharted frontiers of geography. He approved the construction of observatories.

Pushed for national research institutions. And in his private diary, he hinted at interest in the "polar anomalies." He wasn't a believer.

But he was listening.

Symmes would never know how close he came. By the mid-1820s, his body was failing. Years of travel, poverty, and public ridicule had eroded his health. Still, he lectured. Still, he wrote. Still, he dreamed of the polar wind in his face, the sky splitting as the Earth welcomed him in.

In 1829, Symmes died in Hamilton, Ohio. He had never seen the Arctic. Never stepped aboard an expedition vessel. Never reached the pole.

But he had lit a fuse.

His followers buried him beneath a modest column. At its peak, they placed a stone globe, cut open at the top like a cracked egg. A monument to a theory most considered nonsense.

But not everyone.

Symmes had a final gift for the nation. A man who'd listened to his lectures, read his writings, and inherited his hunger.

Younger, sharper, politically savvy. A storyteller with fire in his throat and ambition in his spine.

His name was Jeremiah Reynolds.

And unlike Symmes, Reynolds would not ask politely.

He would demand.

Chapter 2: Reynolds' Rise – The Prophet of the Poles

He walked into Charleston like a man with a message and a clock ticking inside his chest.
Jeremiah N. Reynolds wasn't a soldier. He wasn't a scientist.

But he moved with the urgency of both—tight-lipped, sharp-eyed, a satchel full of notes and a voice that could silence a crowd without raising volume. He had arrived to speak. Not about trade. Not about politics. About the ends of the Earth.

The announcement had gone up in the newspapers: a lecture on Polar Geography and the Future of American Exploration.

A few skeptics came expecting to be entertained. Others came ready to jeer. But most were just curious. The room filled. The lamps were lit. The chairs creaked beneath the weight of planters, merchants, naval men, and their sons.

Then Reynolds stepped to the front.

And everything changed.

He didn't shout. He didn't wave props or point to globes. He spoke like a man reading from the edge of a holy text—describing not what had been, but what *could be*. He conjured images of vast southern oceans, of swirling winds and strange birds, of magnetic needles that spun in circles and waters warm where they shouldn't be.

He spoke of a new age of discovery.

Not led by Britain. Not by France.

By *America*.

And in his final breath, he asked the room a question: "Who among you will go where the maps stop lying?"

They didn't clap.

They *stood.*

That night, everything shifted.

Reynolds had studied law, worked as an editor, taught school. But his real education began the day he first heard Symmes speak. He knew the theory was flawed—too literal, too fragile—but beneath the geometry was something more dangerous: belief. Symmes had believed there was another world waiting. Reynolds believed it too. But he didn't need a hole at the poles. He just needed a door.

Jeremiah Reynolds

For nearly a decade, he had wandered the eastern seaboard giving lectures, writing essays, pleading with newspapers to publish his vision. Most thought he was eccentric. Some thought he was brilliant. A few thought he was both.

But by 1834, Reynolds was more than a curiosity.

He was a movement.

In Charleston, he found allies. Wealthy plantation owners, eager to fund an expedition that might open new routes to the East. Naval officers, enticed by the prospect of glory. Even Southern politicians, always eager to stake claims before the

North.

Reynolds seized the moment. He called for a national expedition—not just to explore the Pacific, but to penetrate the mysteries of the Antarctic. To gather specimens. Chart islands.

Record magnetic deviations. But also, between the lines, to follow the echoes of Symmes.

He didn't say it directly.

He didn't *have* to.

He traveled to Washington, spoke with congressmen, pushed for legislation. He lobbied the Secretary of the Navy, appealed to scientific societies, wrote pamphlets designed to circulate among the salons of Philadelphia and the coffeehouses of New York.

He was relentless.

And in 1836, Congress relented.

They approved the creation of an official U.S. exploring expedition. It would be the largest voyage of discovery the young republic had ever undertaken. Six vessels. Hundreds of men.

Dozens of scientists. And a captain named Charles Wilkes—a young but ambitious naval officer with something to prove.

Reynolds should have been on that ship.

He *deserved* to be on that ship.

But the Navy had grown wary. He was too passionate, too political. They feared his lectures, his followers, his baggage. The

Navy wanted clean orders. Controlled headlines.

They cut him.

He didn't protest.

He simply stepped aside, watching as the vessels he had summoned into being were launched without him.

The U.S. Exploring Expedition set sail in 1838. Its official purpose was science. Cartography. Trade. It would map the Pacific, explore the South Seas, and perhaps, if weather allowed, venture toward the Antarctic ice.

But unofficially, it carried a deeper burden.

A whisper.
A theory.
A legacy.

Reynolds stayed behind. For a time. But the fire in him would not go out.

He still believed there were truths buried beneath the ice.

He still believed Symmes had been right about *something*.

And most of all, he believed that knowledge wasn't given.

It was *taken*.

By those willing to go far enough.

Reynolds didn't wait for an invitation.

If they wouldn't let him go under the American flag, he'd go without one. He booked passage aboard a merchant vessel bound for South America, carrying little more than a notebook, a pair of boots, and an unshakable conviction that his time hadn't passed—it had simply shifted latitude.

In Chile, he wandered the harbors and hillsides, taking notes on tides and winds, interviewing sailors who claimed to have seen strange lights beyond the Cape. He bartered his way onto ships heading farther south, writing dispatches to American journals, still shaping the national appetite for exploration even as he stood half a world away from Washington.

In Valparaiso, he boarded a sealer and sailed into the Southern Ocean. The ship creaked and hissed through sleet and fog. The crew laughed at his books but listened when he spoke of currents that didn't follow compass rules, of birds that vanished into the snow, and of heat rising from below the ice.

He never claimed to be following Symmes' path.

But he kept looking south.

And the further south he went, the more the world began to shift under his feet.

The sky sharpened. The cold deepened. And the edge of the known world grew thin.

He saw the icebergs—cathedrals of silence, floating above black depths. He felt the tremor in the ship's hull as it creaked past unknown shoals. He watched the albatross vanish into low clouds, and more than once, he wrote in his journal that the wind carried with it a warmth that *should not exist.*

In one letter, never published but kept in a private archive, he wrote:

"I do not believe the world is hollow. But I do believe it is hiding."

He returned to Valparaiso gaunt, sun-burned, and bone-weary. He was not a young man anymore. The expedition he had envisioned was already underway without him, deep in the Pacific. Wilkes was sailing from island to island, mapping coasts, gathering coral, and slowly pushing the fleet south.

Reynolds took passage back to the United States.

When he arrived in New York, no crowd met him at the dock.

No journalists sought his comment. The spotlight had moved on.

But history hadn't.

Because by 1840, Wilkes and the U.S. Exploring Expedition had reached Antarctica.

And what they found there would ignite new questions.

Not just about ice.

But about *what lay beneath* it.

They sighted land.

Not just icebergs, but coastline—vast, white, and unbroken.

Mountains of ice, cliffs that rose from a sea boiling with storm.

For the first time, American sailors recorded the existence of a southern continent.

But they also recorded other things.

Magnetic variations so severe that compasses spun like clocks. Sudden, inexplicable rises in ocean temperature near ice shelves. Vast caverns glimpsed in glaciers, where the wind blew *warm* from within. They collected rocks unlike any found in the Pacific. Plants trapped in ice that didn't match known species.

And on more than one occasion, they reported hearing sounds beneath the ice—vibrations too rhythmic for shifting glaciers.

The logs don't say Hollow Earth.

They don't mention Symmes.

But they don't need to.

The entries tell a story of confusion, awe, and something like *fear*.

The closer they got to the pole, the stranger everything became.

And then, just as quickly as they had arrived, they turned back.

Wilkes ordered the fleet to pull away. The risk was too high.

Supplies were low. The weather had turned savage. And whether it was the ice, or something else, the expedition retreated—carrying with it a mountain of data, sketches, and sealed reports.

When they returned to America in 1842, they were hailed as heroes.

Maps were redrawn.

Museums overflowed with specimens.

And somewhere in Ohio, the globe atop Symmes' grave caught the morning light.

The holes still faced north and south.

Still open.

Still waiting.

Reynolds never made it to Antarctica.

But he didn't have to.

He had already succeeded.

He had turned a lunatic's cry into a national endeavor. He had raised a generation of explorers who looked at blank space and asked what if. He had transformed the Hollow Earth from a joke into a riddle—and passed it off to men with ships, guns, and the American flag.

In his final years, he returned to writing, spinning stories of whalers and storms and islands that didn't exist on any official charts. His works inspired writers like Poe and Melville. He faded into literary footnotes.

But those who knew—those who had heard him speak, read his reports, felt the fire behind his ideas—they remembered.

He didn't find the Hollow Earth.

He found something *better*.

He proved that even in a nation addicted to certainty, there was still room for the impossible.

As long as someone was willing to chase it.

Chapter 3: A President's Ear – The Hollow Earth in the White House

It took years. Speeches, pamphlets, editorials. But Reynolds' fire caught. His words echoed in navy halls, in congressional backrooms, in the minds of a restless young nation eager to carve its place on the global stage. And in 1838, the dream became steel.

They launched six ships. Reynold's wasn't on board, but his ideas were.

Washington D.C. was still half-mud when John Quincy Adams took the oath of office. The streets weren't paved. The White House was drafty. The Capitol dome hadn't yet risen. It wasn't a city of power—it was a skeleton of ambition, bones waiting for flesh. But inside its halls walked a man who believed, with the quiet fury of a scholar, that America's destiny wasn't just to grow—it was to know.

Adams had spent his life in books and embassies. He read Latin at eight. Was ambassador to the Netherlands by twenty-six. Served in the Senate, the State Department, and now, as president, he brought to the office a mind sharp enough to terrify mo st of Congress. He kept diaries, thousands of pages long. He measured his own failures with brutal clarity.
And yet—behind the stately sentences and stiff posture—there lived something wild.

Curiosity.

He believed the Earth still held secrets. That the poles were not frozen boundaries but *questions*. That the stars above and the ice below were meant to be charted, understood, maybe even claimed.

U.S. President Adams

So when word reached his desk that a man named Symmes was declaring the Earth hollow and offering to lead an expedition into the unknown, Adams didn't laugh.

He paused.

And he listened.

Symmes hadn't made it easy. His theory was bizarre, his evidence flimsy, his personality brittle. But his passion was undeniable. By 1823, he had followers—men like James McBride, who petitioned Congress with a formal request: fund a polar expedition. Equip a crew. Head north. Find the hole.

It wasn't a joke.

It was filed, debated, and recorded.

They didn't approve it.

But they didn't burn it either.

That alone was remarkable.

Adams didn't endorse the theory. He didn't fund the mission.
But he did something far more dangerous: he let the question
hang in the air. He never dismissed it outright. And in doing
so, he gave it space to grow.

He'd seen enough in his life to know that today's fantasy could
become tomorrow's fact. He'd seen Jefferson send Lewis and

Clark into an uncharted wilderness with a blank map and a
stack of dreams. He'd watched Napoleon fall, steam power
rise, and the line between science and story blur again and
again.

He knew that ridicule wasn't proof.

It was often camouflage.

So when Symmes' supporters knocked at the gates of the republic with maps and models, Adams didn't open the door—
but he didn't lock it either.

He left it ajar.

And others noticed.

Naval officers began discussing the strange reports from Arctic
whalers—unseasonably warm air near the ice, strange magnetic
interference, birds vanishing into the polar sky. Explorers
spoke of mirages, drifting icebergs that seemed to emerge from
nowhere, and curiously colored skies.

It wasn't confirmation.

But it was fuel.

Reynolds was already fanning the flames.

He'd taken up Symmes' mantle, but with polish and fire. Where Symmes had sounded like a man possessed, Reynolds spoke like a prophet. He turned Hollow Earth into poetry. A song of the unknown. A hymn to the last blank corners of the Earth. He wrote articles that blended science, myth, and nationalism. He lectured with the precision of a scientist and the rhythm of a revivalist preacher. And in every word, he invoked the same idea:

We must *go*.

Not because we are certain—but because we are not.
Adams watched it unfold. He had other battles—internal improvements, tariffs, slavery—but the call to exploration stirred something in him. He had wanted to build a national observatory, a university, a network of scientific institutions that would rival Europe. He had failed on many fronts. His enemies called him cold, remote, even arrogant. But they misunderstood him.

He wasn't aloof.

He was looking *further*.

He believed the mind was a frontier. And that America, if it was to survive its own violence and greed, would have to become a nation of minds, not just muskets.

He supported polar observation.

He encouraged scientific societies.

And he gave space for men like Reynolds to speak.

It didn't last.

In 1828, Adams lost the presidency to Andrew Jackson, a war hero who despised academics and didn't trust any idea that couldn't be shot at or bought. Jackson dismantled half of Adams' projects. He gutted the observatory plan. He ignored the polar petitions.

And in the winter of that transition, the door began to close.

But not entirely.
Because ideas don't die when the man who listens to them leaves office.

They wait.

In letters.

In rumors.

In sealed orders.

And somewhere—among the books Adams packed as he left the White House—was a note scribbled in his own hand.

It read:

"No truth is ridiculed more violently than that which stands just beyond the veil of understanding."

He never said what it referred to.

But he didn't have to.

John Quincy Adams didn't just leave office. He reentered the battlefield.

Most men who lost the presidency faded into countryside obscurity or went abroad to nurse their dignity. Not Adams. He went to Congress. The only former president ever to do so. He returned not as a statesman above the fray, but as a warrior on the floor—armed with papers, memory, and an almost painful devotion to principle. He didn't care for popularity. He didn't need allies. He had ideas.

And one of those ideas had always been the pursuit of knowledge, no matter how strange the path.

In the halls of Congress, he fought for education, scientific investment, and the freedom of thought. He quoted from ancient texts and new journals, arguing that discovery was not a luxury but a national imperative. The republic, he said, would rise or fall not on its borders, but on its *questions*.

And some of those questions pointed toward the poles.

The theory of Hollow Earth never became policy. But it lingered like mist around a lantern—always just at the edge of the respectable conversation. It had entered the bloodstream of a new kind of American mythology. Not because it was true. But because it was bold.

The Navy knew it.

The intellectual circles of the Eastern seaboard whispered about it.

Even European scientists, some of whom dismissed Symmes outright, privately admitted they had no explanation for certain polar anomalies. The warmth of Arctic currents. The compass needles that danced without cause. The flocks of geese seen disappearing into the northern sky—never to return.

There was no proof.

But there was just enough *strangeness* to keep the question alive.

And Reynolds, always watching, always calculating, knew exactly how to use it.

He was now more than a lecturer. He was a force. His writings appeared in the *Southern Literary Messenger*, *New York Mirror*, and other journals that walked the line between science and cultural commentary. He repackaged the Hollow Earth as a symbol—not of madness, but of mystery. He invoked the ghost of Symmes not as a warning, but as a challenge.

The frontier, he said, was no longer where the maps ended.

It was where the facts failed.

In 1836, nearly two decades after Symmes stood on his crate in St. Louis, Reynolds watched as the United States finally approved the creation of a formal naval expedition. It would explore the Pacific. Chart Antarctica. Gather scientific data. It would be America's first voyage of discovery on a global scale.

It was everything he had fought for.

And they left him behind.

The Navy cut him from the final roster. No official explanation was ever recorded. Some said he was too political. Too controversial. A civilian liability. Others whispered that he was still seen as tainted by Symmes' madness. Whatever the truth, Reynolds was denied the one thing he'd given years of his life to achieve.

But he didn't rage.

He disappeared into the shadows.

And the expedition set sail.

Six ships.

Over 300 men.

A mission that would span four years, circle the globe, and change the map of the world forever.

They were called the United States Exploring Expedition.

The Ex. Ex.

Their goals were scientific.

But their cargo included something far more dangerous than microscopes and specimen jars.

They carried the remnants of a dream.

A theory that had once reached the president's ear.

And now moved in the sealed compartments of the human imagination.

Adams, old and growing frail, knew about the mission. He didn't speak of it in public, but in private letters he expressed quiet pride. It had taken longer than it should. It had left behind the man who had lit the fire. But it was *happening*.

The nation was going.

And it was going *south*.

Toward the ice.
Toward the edge.

Toward the place where questions turned into myth—and myth into revelation.

Symmes was dead. Buried beneath a monument few visited.

Reynolds was in exile, wandering South America, writing essays no one read. And Adams was near the end of his life.

But something had begun.

The ships cut through the Atlantic like scalpels.

And whether the officers aboard believed in Hollow Earth or not, they carried the weight of an idea that had haunted a generation.

That the Earth still held secrets.

And that somewhere near the bottom of the world, the door might still be open.

Chapter 4: Voyage of the Peacock – The Expedition Begins

She sat in harbor like a predator at rest.

The USS *Peacock*, her hull dark with fresh pitch, masts rising like bayonets into the sky, was not the largest of the six ships commissioned for the U.S. Exploring Expedition—but she was the heart. A sloop-of-war, fast and lean, built for maneuvering into tight waters and away from threats with equal speed. Beneath her decks, she carried not just guns and rations, but the weight of a nation's first great scientific gamble.

The year was 1838.

The United States was only sixty years old.

But it was about to look outward.

The *Peacock* would lead a fleet that included the *Vincennes, Porpoise, Sea Gull, Flying Fish,* and *Relief.* Together they made up the most ambitious maritime endeavor in American history—part science, part statecraft, and, quietly, part *search*. The mission was clear: chart the South Pacific, study flora and fauna, collect minerals and magnetic readings. That was what the papers said.

But the men aboard knew there was something else.

They had read the lectures.

Heard the rumors.

And a few, just a few, believed.

That somewhere near the pole, the Earth held a secret.

And that they were sailing straight toward it.

Charles Wilkes stood at the bow of the *Vincennes*, the flagship of the fleet, squinting into the horizon as the final lines were cast off. He was young—barely forty—and small in stature, but driven by something sharp and cold beneath the surface. He had lobbied hard for this command. Fought rivals. Survived politics. He believed in measurement, precision, and command.

He also knew the mission's deeper current.

He had read Symmes. He had heard Reynolds speak. And though he never claimed to endorse the Hollow Earth, he had once written, in a private letter, that the poles remained "matters not yet resolved."

It was a diplomatic phrase.

But it left room.

Room for questions.

Room for wonder.

Room for fear.

The fleet slipped out of Norfolk in August, their sails swelling with a wind that seemed, for once, to know where it was going. Officers leaned over railings, watching the coastline recede. Below deck, sailors jostled for space in cramped hammocks, grumbled over stale bread, and whispered about what lay ahead.

No one knew what to expect.

Their charts were patchy at best. Entire swaths of the Pacific were still drawn with dotted lines and speculative names. "Danger Reef." "Cannibal Coast." "Ice Barrier—impassable." Some of the officers joked that they were following ghosts.

Others, more quietly, studied the readings—barometers, compasses, thermometers—looking for anomalies.

They didn't have GPS.

They had stars and instinct.

And something else.

The sealed orders.

They wouldn't be opened until the fleet passed Brazil.

They were locked in a brass case, marked for Wilkes' eyes only.

And whatever they contained, it wasn't in the newspapers.

By the time they reached Rio de Janeiro, three men had already gone mad.

Not violently—yet—but with the dull, smothering madness of isolation and heat. One had stripped naked and tried to climb the rigging. Another claimed to see shadows beneath the waves, shapes that followed them no matter their heading. The third simply stopped speaking, staring southward for hours on end.

Wilkes logged it all.

Lt Charles Wilkes

He was a man of order, but even he had begun to notice things.

The ocean temperatures were inconsistent. Warmer than they should be. One morning, the *Porpoise* reported its compass spinning for four minutes before stabilizing. That same evening, a sailor swore the moon set twice.

Wilkes blamed weather. Fatigue.

But he didn't throw the reports away.

He filed them.

Catalogued them.

And said nothing.

In Rio, the fleet reprovisioned. Fresh water, salted meat, fruit, new rope. The officers dined in colonial salons, posed for sketches, sent letters back home. But beneath the civility, there was tension. Some of the junior officers had begun arguing over the secondary purpose of the voyage. Not openly—but in hushed tones, in corners.

One lieutenant, a cartographer from Massachusetts, had brought with him a copy of Reynolds' *Address on the Subject of a Surveying and Exploring Expedition*. He read from it one night, by candlelight, as four others sat close, the wind snapping through the open gunports.

He read the line aloud:

"If we are to become a people worthy of history's gaze, we must go where others dare not."

No one spoke.

Then someone said: "What if there really is an opening?"

And someone else: "Wouldn't we already know?"

The cartographer smiled. "Would we?"

The fleet left Rio under heavy skies.

The orders were opened.

And though the contents were never fully revealed to the public, those close to Wilkes noted a change in him afterward.

He grew quieter.
More focused.

He held long meetings with his senior officers. Plotted new courses. Made adjustments to the supply logs.

And when one of the scientists asked why they were scheduled to sail farther south than expected before heading west toward the Pacific, Wilkes only said:

"We're going to verify some theories."

He never said which ones.
He didn't have to.

The wind was shifting.

The sea was changing.

And the southern ice—still weeks away—was already casting its shadow over the fleet.

They cut across the Atlantic like ghost ships.

The winds stiffened, the temperatures dropped. White squalls sprang up out of nowhere and vanished just as quickly, like nature was toying with them. The rigging froze at night. Salt stuck to eyebrows and canvas like hoarfrost. The *Peacock* led the charge, her dark hull breaking through waves that grew steeper and stranger the farther south they sailed.

Then came the fog.

Dense, endless, clinging to the fleet like wet wool. Sunlight became a theory. Sailors groped through the decks like blind men.

The compass needles quivered. Lanterns burned green. Time stretched. Morale thinned.

Still they sailed.

Lieutenant Wilkes made his men keep meticulous logs—barometric pressure, wind speed, magnetic drift, ocean depth, cloud formations. He had them record everything. But there were entries he didn't send back to Washington. Pages torn out.

Words redacted. Notes locked in his personal chest. The ones that didn't make sense.

Sailors hearing music through the fog.
Shadowy shapes seen moving under the ice floes.

A warm breeze blowing across the deck at 3 a.m., when the sky above was clear and the water below was frozen black.

One midshipman claimed he saw lights dancing along the horizon like a string of fireflies. Wilkes dismissed it as Aurora Australis. But even he knew they were still far from the magnetic zone.

And the lights moved *too low*.

They reached the edge of the Antarctic Circle on a moonless night.

No one spoke when they crossed the line. There were no cheers, no toasts. Only silence and the sound of ice scraping the hull. The lookouts doubled their shifts. The crows' nests were manned constantly. Below deck, the naturalists secured their specimens and began to pack them away—just in case.

Wilkes issued orders: head deeper.

The *Peacock* led the advance, skimming along the fringe of the frozen sea. They were looking for a passage—something that might break open the white wall stretching endlessly across the horizon. What they found was something else.

A gap.

Not large, but unmistakable. A deep blue channel between the ice shelves. Water flowing *into* it. Warmer than the sea around it. Steam curling upward.

The scientists noted the change immediately. The air smelled different. Metallic. The temperature was five degrees higher than expected. Ice on the rigging melted in rivulets. One sailor took off his gloves.

Then they heard it.

A low, rhythmic thrum, like distant thunder—but steady. It came from *beneath* the water.

Wilkes didn't give a speech.

He just gave an order.

They would follow the channel.

The *Peacock* crept forward, its hull groaning with every shift in the current. The other ships held back—only the *Flying Fish*, a smaller tender, followed close. The walls of ice rose on either side, forty feet high and glittering like crushed glass. Snow fell upward in gusts. The sky disappeared.

Still the water warmed.

At one point, the needle on the ship's thermometer bent *backwards*, curling like it had been struck with heat.

They reached a dead end.

Or what looked like one.

A vast wall of ice, as smooth as glass and curved—*unnaturally curved*. No cracks, no jagged breaks. Just a dome of frost. The water pooled in front of it, bubbling gently. The thrum had stopped.

Wilkes ordered soundings.

No bottom.

Eighty fathoms.

Then one hundred.

Then nothing.

The line went slack. As if the ocean simply opened beneath them.

No one spoke of Hollow Earth.

No one had to.

They anchored in the channel for three nights. On the second, the stars vanished completely, as though the sky had shut its eyes. The fog returned. The air tasted of copper. And the sound came back—fainter now, but pulsing in rhythm with the waves.

On the third night, a man went missing.

Quartermaster Doyle. He had been on watch.

His gloves were found on deck.

His coat was folded neatly on a coil of rope.

But no footprints.
No splash.

He had simply vanished.

The logs mention a "presumed fall," but no one believed that.
The sailors stopped sleeping.

The officers stopped writing.

And Wilkes gave the order to turn back.

The *Peacock* rejoined the fleet at the edge of the ice shelf.

Wilkes reported the "false channel" as a dead lead.

He noted magnetic variations and unusual temperatures.

He made no mention of the sound.

No mention of Doyle.
No mention of the dome.

But something changed in him.

He kept to his cabin more often.

His orders became more cautious, but less rational. He delayed movements. Redrew charts. And when asked by one of his lieutenants what exactly they had seen down there, Wilkes only replied:

"We weren't supposed to be there."

And then he said nothing else.

They sailed west after that.

Away from the ice.

Away from the questions.

The fleet scattered across the Pacific, each ship following new orders—Samoa, Fiji, Tahiti, Hawaii.

They became explorers again.

Scientists.

Cartographers.

But deep in the heart of every logbook was a silent entry, unwritten but understood.

That at the bottom of the world, past the cold and the dark and the edge of the known, the Earth had whispered something back.

And none of them wanted to hear it again.

Chapter 5: Across the Pacific – Into the Floating World

The ice receded behind them like a bad dream.
As the fleet turned northwest, the sails caught warmer winds. The ships rolled easier. Faces that had been pinched by cold and fear slowly relaxed in the sun. By the time they reached Tahiti, the horror of the southern channel had become something less than a memory—less than a secret. It became *unspoken.*

But it never left them.

The South Pacific stretched out before them like a storybook turned sideways. Islands dotted the sea like scattered jewels— each with its own language, climate, kingdom, and current. There was trade to be done. Specimens to collect. Charts to draw. And yet, for the men of the U.S. Exploring Expedition, something had shifted.

This was no longer just a voyage of science.

They had seen something beneath the world.

Now they were trying to forget.

Wilkes gave no indication that the experience had changed him. His reports grew more meticulous. His discipline, more severe. He reprimanded officers for minor delays. Confiscated unauthorized sketches. He insisted that the polar incident had been meteorological—a pressure anomaly, a navigational mistake. But even he couldn't explain the warmth. Or the sound.

Or why his men had started muttering in their sleep.

When the *Peacock* reached the Society Islands, the crew was exhausted but restless. The tropical beauty did little to soothe their nerves. The locals welcomed them with garlands and songs. The naturalists began collecting specimens—new birds, new shells, new diseases. But there was a tension in the fleet.

A taut silence beneath the surface.

Lieutenant Knox of the *Flying Fish* wrote in his private journal:

"We are men of science, yes, but we are also men of shadow now. We have touched something we cannot name. I believe the Earth is stranger than we thought. And I fear the captain knows more than he tells."

Still, the work went on.

They mapped atolls that no European had ever recorded. Measured the depths of lagoons. Sketched coastlines by lantern light. In Tonga, they witnessed a royal funeral. In Fiji, they bartered for breadfruit and buried a man who had died of fever.

On every island, the locals offered stories—legends of gods who lived beneath the sea, of fires that burned under the mountains, of birds that vanished into the earth.

The Americans smiled.

Took notes.

Laughed politely.

But they had heard those stories before.

And they sounded *different* now.

In Samoa, a native priest told Wilkes that the ocean itself was alive. That it opened and closed like a mouth. That ships could be swallowed whole, not by storms, but by the breathing of the Earth. Wilkes thanked him. Offered tobacco. Wrote down nothing.

That night, three of the sailors requested transfers.

One deserted entirely.

He was never found.

Wilkes made no mention of it in the logs.

For all their discipline and Enlightenment training, the officers of the Ex. Ex. had begun to fracture into two camps.

There were those who believed the anomalies of Antarctica were explainable—glacial pressure, optical illusions, magnetic fields. They were the men who kept to the science, to the specimens, to the books. They worked harder now. As if to build a wall between themselves and the thing they couldn't explain.

And then there were the others.

The quiet ones.

The ones who watched the horizon a little too long.

Who whispered when the wind changed.

Who began to believe that the expedition hadn't *left* the unknown—it had *entered* it.

Reynolds had warned them, years before. The poles were only the beginning. The real mystery wasn't where the Earth ended. It was where it *opened*.

And now, thousands of miles from that icy wall, they began to wonder whether that opening wasn't limited to one place.

Whether it might... move.

Whether it might *follow*.

In Tahiti, Wilkes met with a British officer from a surveying vessel. The two exchanged pleasantries, compared notes, traded charts. The Brit offered rum. Wilkes declined. Then he asked a question, almost offhand:

"Have you encountered any unusual... fluctuations? Compass errors?"

The Brit raised an eyebrow.

"We had one, near the Marquesas. Needle spun for a full minute. Thought it was a defect. But—" he paused. "You've seen it too, haven't you?"

Wilkes didn't answer.

He only nodded.

And left.

The Pacific was supposed to be mapped, measured, named.

But instead, the deeper they went, the more it slipped away.

The constellations didn't change, but the air did. The winds carried scents that didn't belong to any island. The birds flew in strange patterns. The stars flickered when they shouldn't.

And always—always—there was that sound.

Low.
Subsonic.

Beneath the hearing.

But felt in the ribs.

It came in waves.
And no one talked about it.

They reached the Marquesas in the dead calm of early September.

The heat was heavy, like a quilt soaked in saltwater. The ships barely moved. The sails sagged. The men sweltered in their uniforms. But the islands were lush, the harbors deep, and the days passed with the dull rhythm of a fleet waiting for wind. It should have been restful.

Instead, it was unnerving.

Each day, the crew logged more inconsistencies. Wind patterns that didn't match barometric pressure. Tides that shifted without reason. Marine life behaving oddly—dolphins circling the hulls at night, flying fish beaching themselves en masse. There was talk of tremors. The helmsman aboard the *Porpoise* claimed he felt the ship "tilt," though the sea was flat.

They checked the instruments.

Everything read normal.

Except nothing felt that way.

Wilkes paced the *Vincennes* like a man stalking a memory. His officers were used to his temper, but now there was something else behind his eyes—an absence, like he was staring through people instead of at them. He slept little. He wrote less. And he avoided the water. The captain who had once taken deep readings with his own hands now refused to lean over the rail.

He knew something.

Or feared something.

And the men noticed.

They stopped asking questions.
They started looking down.

From the Marquesas they sailed to Fiji, where the reception was colder. Cannibal raids had occurred inland days before.

The chiefs were wary. The naturalists collected what they could, but many stayed aboard. The jungle seemed to breathe, and not in a comforting way. One sailor said he felt like the trees were "watching us back."

They took on fruit. Water. News.

More legends.

Every island had them.

Stories of gods that came from inside the mountains. Birds that flew underground. A hole in the sea that could swallow an entire fleet and spit it out in another world. It would have been amusing if it hadn't sounded like everything they weren't saying about Antarctica.

No one mentioned the hole.

But no one laughed at it either.

Then came the dream.

It spread through the *Peacock* first, then the *Flying Fish*, then to the *Relief*. Officers, sailors, even the ship's cook reported it: standing at the edge of an icy shelf, staring into a void, wind rushing upward from beneath, and something—a voice?—calling in a language no one could place.

Not all on the same night.

Not even all in the same form.

But the theme was the same.

Openings.

Descent.

Sound.

Wilkes claimed he didn't dream.

But he began keeping a second logbook, one he locked away.

And he altered the route.

The new course would take them farther west—deeper into Micronesia.

On paper, it was to chart lesser-known reefs.

But some of the officers suspected he was looking for something else.

Something *familiar.*

In Guam, they found a British whaler anchored offshore with a shattered foremast. The crew looked ragged, haunted. Wilkes sent a boarding party. What they learned was fragmentary— shouted over waves, muttered over shared tea.

The British ship had tried to chart an unrecorded current near the Caroline Islands. They had followed warm water in a region that should have been cold. At night, they heard low frequencies echoing through the hull. Then, for three hours, every compass on board reversed polarity. They turned back. A week later, a squall blew out their mast.

One of the British sailors, wild-eyed and sleepless, asked a petty officer from the *Peacock* a single question:
"Do your bones hum?"

No one spoke of it after.

By late November, the fleet had reached the Philippines.

A storm delayed them at sea for days—hurricane winds, rogue waves. The *Sea Gull* nearly capsized. But when it passed, they found something stranger than wreckage.

All six ships reported the same phenomenon.

The temperature dropped sharply—by almost twenty degrees. The sea turned still. And the sky went white—not cloudy, not fogged, just white. A blank canvas of light. It lasted six minutes.

The sun was gone. The stars vanished. And the compasses all pointed down.

Then, without warning, everything returned to normal. Wilkes ordered silence.

No mention of the event in any official logs.

But the men talked.

Whispers spread through the hammocks and wardrooms.

Had they passed over a fault?

A crater?

A hole?

Someone said it out loud once—and was put in irons for three days.

There was a pattern forming.

Heat where there should be cold. Magnetic shifts where the Earth should be steady. And stories, everywhere, of openings. Not just at the poles.

But in the sea.

In the sky.

In the *mind*.

The Hollow Earth was no longer a theory from a lecture hall.

It was becoming a *presence*.

Not a place.

A pressure.

Something that moved beneath the expedition like a tide.

Wilkes didn't write about it.

But the sailors could feel it.

The ocean had changed.
And the men had changed with it.

Chapter 6: The Hidden Mission – What They Were Really Looking For

The order was unsealed at midnight.

The fleet had just dropped anchor off the coast of Borneo. The heat lay thick over the water like oil, but the sea was oddly calm. That night, in the lantern-lit wardroom of the *Vincennes*, Lieutenant Charles Wilkes unlocked the brass box that had remained unopened since the expedition departed American shores. It was bound in navy wax and stamped with the seal of the Secretary of the Navy.

There were four pages.

The first three outlined official instructions—new targets for magnetic surveys, corrections to the Pacific charting schedule, directives to coordinate with British vessels in the East Indies. But the fourth sheet was different. No header. No signature.

Just a handwritten memorandum, in tight, formal script.

Proceed at your discretion to high southern latitudes. Investigate reports of geothermal anomalies, magnetic irregularities, and unusual oceanographic readings. Do not publish data until reviewed.

That was all.

No explanation.

No author.

But Wilkes understood.

He had always known there was more to this mission than starfish and coral.

Now it was official.

The Navy didn't believe in Hollow Earth. Not exactly. But they *suspected* something was happening in the polar regions—something outside the limits of accepted science. Whether they hoped for new trade routes, exotic minerals, or simple military advantage, Wilkes didn't know. But the instruction was clear:

Find the anomaly.

And don't talk about it.

He summoned his senior officers one by one. No group meetings. No discussion. Each man received his instructions alone, behind closed doors. Most accepted without question. Some blinked, nodded, and left quickly. One—a young lieutenant from Boston—asked a single question:

"Sir, if we find something... what then?"

Wilkes didn't answer.
He dismissed the man without a word.

The route changed again.

No explanation was given.

The *Peacock*, *Flying Fish*, and *Porpoise* were assigned new survey areas near New Guinea. The *Vincennes* would take a narrow circuit near the Solomon Islands. The *Sea Gull* and *Relief* were ordered to remain in port for resupply and repairs.

But all of them—quietly, subtly—were directed to begin collecting specific data:

Subsurface temperatures.

Unusual currents.

Atmospheric pressure deviations.

Compass drift in mid-ocean latitudes.

And every sailor on every ship was told, without ceremony, that new codes were now in effect. Certain reports would be sealed. New logs would be written in duplicate—one copy for the Navy, one for the public record.

No one said "classified."

The word didn't yet exist.

But the silence was the same.

The first major reading came off the coast of New Caledonia. At dawn, the *Flying Fish* recorded a spike in water temperature over a deep trench—seven degrees above average. The crew thought it was a broken instrument. They recalibrated. Took readings again. Same result. They dropped a lead line.

The rope came back steaming.

No one believed it.

But it was logged.

That same day, the *Peacock*—over two hundred nautical miles away—recorded a magnetic surge that threw the compass ten degrees off. The helmsman assumed a mechanical failure. He reset it. The error returned. They dropped anchor and drifted.

By midnight, the compass righted itself.

But the wind died completely.

And in the stillness, the crew heard a sound—deep, low, and endless.

As if the sea itself were inhaling.

Back on the *Vincennes*, Wilkes read the reports without comment.

He lit his lantern. Reviewed his personal logbook. Sketched a new map.

He plotted each anomaly—heat, magnetism, drift.

When he was done, he sat back and stared at the pattern.

It formed a spiral.

A tight, uncoiling spiral over the southern ocean.

He didn't sleep that night.

In the weeks that followed, the fleet continued its revised course.

Officially, they charted coral reefs and recorded species. Unofficially, they hunted whispers. Any sign of subterranean vents.

Any thermal spike. Any compass misbehavior.

And always—always—that sound returned.

Different ships.

Different nights.

Same tone.

Like a great engine turning far below the world.

Sailors began reporting pressure in their ears.

Dreams became vivid.

A few began to sketch spirals in their journals, unaware others were doing the same.

They didn't call it Hollow Earth.

But it was hollowing *them*.

One night, off the coast of Bougainville, a storm rose without warning. Lightning hit the mast of the *Porpoise*. The ship listed, then righted. As they fought to recover, the lookout screamed—he had seen land where no land was charted. A rocky outcropping. A cliff face. Black as coal and slick with sea.

They turned to pursue.

There was nothing there.
Only mist.
And the sea.
And the sound.

The crew of the *Peacock* began to change.

It wasn't mutiny. Not yet. But the transformation was visible—in the way they spoke less, slept less, watched the sea more. The ship doctor noted more headaches, nosebleeds, complaints of pressure behind the eyes. One sailor claimed his dreams no longer belonged to him. Another carved spirals into his bunk post, dozens of them, as though compelled.

No one said Hollow Earth.

But it was no longer a theory.

It was an *influence*.

A low, ambient vibration running through the voyage like a hidden current.

Wilkes increased discipline. Issued double watches. Confiscated private sketches. He grew paranoid about the naturalists and their field journals. He demanded copies of their notes, redacted anything he deemed speculative, and warned them not to publish until "full review by the Department."

One geologist asked, flatly, "Are we still mapping the world, or trying to hide it?"

Wilkes discharged him at the next port.

The man vanished without a trace.

In early January, the *Flying Fish* encountered a curious for-mation—a series of submerged islets, perfectly round, un-charted on any known map. They called them "The Marbles."

Their sonar readings—primitive but effective—indicated hol-low pockets beneath the reef. When they dropped lead lines, the water turned cloudy. Some of the crew claimed the ocean *tasted different.*

The next day, their chronometers failed.
Every clock on the ship lost seven minutes.

Not at once.

Gradually.

As though time itself had been… *interfered with.*
They didn't talk about it on the record.

But one officer wrote privately,
"We are drifting not through geography, but through myth."

Meanwhile, the *Vincennes* intercepted a French merchant vessel limping westward from New Zealand. Its crew had a look Wilkes recognized—tired, sunburned, but mostly hollow-eyed.

They had sailed too far south, chasing a new whaling lane.

What they found, they said, was a fog bank that never lifted.

Warm water where ice should have been. And a horizon that *bent.*

The French captain said only this:
"There is something beneath."

Then he handed Wilkes a stone—black, smooth, veined with gold. It had been found floating alone in the sea, as if pushed upward by a current with no source.

The *Vincennes'* geologist couldn't identify the composition.

It wasn't volcanic.

It wasn't coral.
It didn't match any known classification.

Wilkes kept it in his personal desk.

And didn't speak of it again.

By now, the patterns were impossible to ignore.

Heat spikes.

Compass drift.

Tidal reversals.

Anomalies that defied their training.

The fleet should have fractured.

Instead, it quieted.

Like men preparing for something they couldn't name.

Orders were passed without voice. Journals went unwritten.

Even the marine artists began sketching more abstractly—shadows beneath the waves, holes in the sky, geometric patterns rising from the sea.

The expedition's official reports continued, full of data and observation.

But the real story was happening in the margins.

In the sealed logs.

In the midnight meetings.

In the *pause* between normal and not.

Then came the incident at Temotu.

A small volcanic island, mostly uninhabited.

The *Peacock* anchored offshore while a shore party investigated signs of geothermal activity. What they found was a cave system—natural, but unnaturally shaped. Hexagonal walls.

Smooth floors. Patterns carved into the stone that no known civilization had ever used.

In the deepest chamber, the air was *hot*—over 100 degrees. But the walls were covered in frost.

The men heard whispers.

The captain of the shore party later shot himself aboard the *Peacock* without explanation.

His suicide note was one word.
"Listening."

Wilkes finally ordered the fleet to regroup.

All ships converged near Papua New Guinea. No reason was given. Only an order: assemble.

The officers gathered in the wardroom of the *Vincennes*. Some had lost weight. Others had begun twitching when the wind shifted. Wilkes entered holding the sealed memorandum—creased now, ink faded—and placed it on the table.

"We've followed the orders," he said.

"We've found the anomalies. The data is sufficient."

A long silence.

Then he added, "We are turning north. This mission is over."

No one objected.
Not because they agreed.
But because they knew.

Whatever they had been chasing—or whatever had been chasing *them*—it wasn't meant to be found.

Not yet.

The fleet began its slow arc northward.

Toward Micronesia.

Toward Manila.

Toward home.

The journals became more scientific again.

The reports more routine.

But beneath the surface, nothing had returned to normal.
Not the crew.

Not the ships.

And certainly not Wilkes.

In his private log, Wilkes wrote:

"We are not explorers. We are trespassers. There is something under the world. It moves. It breathes. And it watches. I will deliver the data. But I will not ask for a second voyage."

He closed the book.
Locked it away.

And set a course for Hawaii.

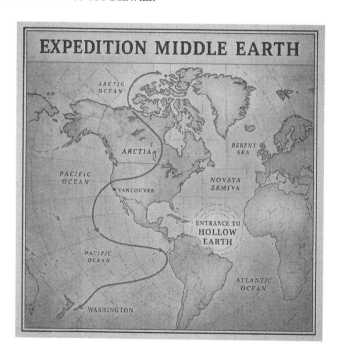

Chapter 7: The Antarctic Barrier – The Edge of the Known World

The fog peeled back like a curtain.

And there it was.

A wall of ice—forty miles wide, a thousand feet high. It rose from the ocean with impossible verticality, a frozen cliff that looked less like a natural formation and more like the rampart of some ancient fortress. No shelves, no slopes, no sign of erosion. Just a gleaming, solid face of white-blue silence, streaked with shadow and light.

The men of the *Peacock* stood along the rails, staring in silence. A few lowered their eyes. Others whispered prayers.

They had reached Antarctica.

And it did not welcome them.

It watched.

The fleet had reassembled at the edge of the southern continent, battered from the Pacific leg, stripped of illusion. They had seen things—heard things—that science couldn't smooth away. But this was something else. This was final. A limit. The true bottom of the world.

The *Vincennes* led the approach.

Wilkes stood at the bow, hands clasped behind his back, coat pulled tight against the wind. His face was pale, unreadable. The official goal was to survey the ice shelf—to confirm what earlier explorers had suspected: that there was land beneath all this white.

But unofficially, they had come to answer another question.

Not "Is there a continent?"

But "What's beneath it?"

They didn't speak it aloud.

But they all felt it.

The temperature dropped fast—faster than expected. The ink
in the pens froze. Eyelids crusted in minutes. Compasses spun

without order. The air itself seemed to thicken. Every foot forward felt like trespass.

They sent out small boats—rowing parties armed with measurement tools, chisels, journals. They took ice samples.

Mapped the cliff line. Looked for entry points. The surface was too sheer. There was no obvious cave, no visible tunnel. But the sound was back.

A hum beneath the water.

A frequency no ear could isolate but every body could feel.

It pulsed beneath their feet.

One seaman from the *Porpoise* dropped to his knees and vomited without warning.

Two others developed nosebleeds.

The doctor called it pressure sickness.

But no barometer showed a shift.

On the second day, they found it.

Not an opening.

Not exactly.
A crack.
Thin, vertical, hundreds of feet high.

It ran along the base of the cliff like a seam in glass.

The temperature near the fissure was twenty degrees warmer.

And from within it, came steam.

They lowered a thermometer.

It came back scalding.

No volcanic activity had ever been reported in that region. No geothermal hotspot mapped. But something was radiating heat from inside the ice.

Wilkes gave no order.

He only said: "We stay."

The *Peacock* remained anchored just offshore.

Each night, strange sounds echoed through the hull—low groans, like something massive shifting beneath them. The ice cracked in patterns too rhythmic to be natural. Some of the crew refused to sleep. One man tried to jump overboard, convinced "they" were calling to him.

He was restrained.

But he wasn't the only one hearing voices.

The men began to report identical dreams: walking through tunnels of ice lit from within by a dull glow, no source, just ambient light. The dreams always ended the same way—with a downward fall into a spiral, and a sense of something massive just ahead, just out of reach.

One lieutenant described it as "falling into a memory the world forgot."

Another refused to describe it at all.

Wilkes recorded none of this in the official logs.
But he wrote in his personal journal:

"We have reached the barrier. But it is not a wall. It is a gate."

By day five, the pressure on the ships had begun to warp the hulls.

Creaking wood. Frost splitting the beams. Instruments failing.

The *Flying Fish* lost a mast in a sudden windless jolt. No one could explain it.

The senior officers met in secret.

They wanted to leave.

Wilkes listened, nodded.

And then said one word:
"No."

He ordered a landing party.

They would approach the crack.

On foot.

Climb the ice.

See where it led.

They didn't know if it would hold.

They didn't know what was inside.

But they had come too far.

Turned away too many times.
There were answers here.

Or madness.

And either one would be a kind of peace.

They set out before dawn.

Six men, roped together, wrapped in oilskins and wool, eyes squinting against the ice-glare. They carried picks, rope, flares, and one pistol—issued quietly by the quartermaster, though no one said why. Wilkes stayed behind on the *Vincennes*, watching from the quarterdeck, lips pressed white. He had chosen the men himself.

They didn't question it.

No one did anymore.

The shoreline was jagged, unnatural. Ice heaved in shelves and cracked with the weight of air alone. Each step forward triggered distant groans, echoes that rolled across the cliffs like cannon fire. But the men pushed on, climbing over sculpted ridges and frozen dunes, always toward the seam—the crack they'd seen from the boats.

It was larger up close.

Easily thirty feet wide at the base, narrowing as it ascended into shadow.

Warm air drifted from its depths.

Steam curled around their boots.

The instruments confirmed it again—unexplainable geothermal activity, no volcanic signature, no logical vent. Just a heat that came from nowhere.

And somewhere deep within…
…the sound.

It pulsed like a second heartbeat, buried under the crust of the world.

The men exchanged glances.

Then entered.

The fissure became a passage.

Not carved—no tool marks, no evidence of human intervention—but unnaturally smooth. The floor sloped downward at an even grade. The walls glistened with frost that never melted, despite the rising warmth. The deeper they went, the easier it became to breathe. No wind. No chill. No echo.

Only that sound.

Not quite a vibration.
Not quite a voice.

A feeling.

Like something waiting.

They descended for what felt like hours, though none of the watches worked anymore. The hands had frozen. Time, it seemed, had lost its authority in this place.

Deep underground all sense of time was lost. Just how far or how deep the team had been descending became a moot point. The air wasn't;'t cold.

 It was warm.
Comfortable.
Soothing.

Then, without warning, the tunnel opened.

The Ex Ex crew found themselves standing in a vast chamber of ice—spherical, domed, radiant from within.

Light shimmered across the walls in rippling hues: pale blue, gold, violet.

No flame.
No sun.

Just ambient luminescence, as if the ice itself remembered sunlight and refused to forget.

In the center of the chamber, the ice had melted into a still pool.

Warm.

Clear.

And bottomless.

One of the men—Lieutenant Hartley—knelt beside it and reached toward the surface.

The others shouted.

Too late.

He touched it.

And whispered something.

They couldn't hear it.

But when he turned, his eyes were wide, pupils pinpricks.

He said, "It's not just hollow."

Then he collapsed.

They carried him out.

He never regained consciousness.

But his pulse remained steady.

His skin, warm.

Almost… too warm.

Like something inside him had changed alignment.

The others said nothing to the officers. Not yet. They claimed an equipment accident. That Hartley had slipped on the ice.

That he'd hit his head.

But that night, each man woke screaming.

Each one saw the same dream.

Spirals.

Descending spirals of light and stone, winding into an endless depth where voices whispered in a language no human throat had ever spoken. Not ancient.

Just *other.*

And when they awoke, each man had a different word written on his palm.

Not ink.
Not blood.

Something else.

It faded by morning.

But the fear did not.

Wilkes interrogated them.

Individually.

He heard their lies.

Read their fear.

And made his decision.

He sealed the entry point.

And ordered explosives.

Not enough to collapse the entire chamber—he couldn't bear that—but enough to seal the path, obscure the seam, erase the descent.

"We weren't meant to go farther," he told the doctor.

"We were meant to see just enough."

The fleet pulled anchor two days later.

No ceremony.
No speeches.

Just the groan of hulls and the silent turning of compasses.

They sailed north into warmer waters.

But the cold stayed inside them.

Hartley never woke.

But he breathed.

Sometimes, when the wind was just right, the men said they could hear him whispering in his sleep. Words they didn't understand.

One of the naturalists, a man trained in Greek, Latin, and Polynesian dialects, tried to transcribe the sounds.

His notes were later destroyed by Wilkes himself.

But before they burned, he told the ship's chaplain one thing:

"It's a map."

They left Antarctica behind.

But they did not escape it.

You don't escape something that was always waiting for you.

You carry it forward.

Into the world.

Into history.

Into the places where science stops and wonder begins.

And behind them, in the great white silence, the crack in the ice began to widen again.

Very slowly.

But steadily.

Like something inside had heard them.

And was beginning to answer.

Chapter 8: The Warm Wind Below – What They Weren't Supposed to Find

They didn't speak of the chamber after they left the ice.

Not on the ships. Not in the logs. Not even in whispers.

But it was there—between them. Inside them. Every gust of wind carried a memory of that heat. Every creak in the hull felt like a breath coming from beneath. They were sailing north, but no one really believed they were moving *away* from anything.

Because it had followed them.

Not a creature. Not a force.

Just the sense of *being seen*.

The *Peacock* pitched forward into gray-green water as they left Antarctic currents behind. The temperature rose. The men stripped off their heavy coats. The ice melted from the decks. Birds reappeared—terns, gulls, albatross.

But the warm wind that rolled across the rails wasn't from the tropics.

It smelled wrong.

Like copper.
Like stone.
Like *depth*.

Hartley still hadn't woken.

They'd moved him to a cot below the infirmary, isolated from the others. His pulse was strong. His skin flushed. But his eyes remained closed. And now, he was humming.

Just low enough to be maddening.

The doctor described it as a kind of resonant muttering—rhythmic, pulsing, like a lullaby from the deep. No one could write it down. The vibrations wouldn't match the page. The sound carried something beneath it. A suggestion. A presence.

They stopped checking on him at night.

They didn't like the way he breathed.

Wilkes began writing letters he never sent.

One addressed to the Secretary of the Navy.

One to his wife.

One—unsigned, unsealed, unaddressed—written entirely in spirals.

The ship's chaplain found him at his desk one morning, eyes sunken, pen motionless. Wilkes stared at a map of the Southern Ocean. Red circles drawn over areas where the instruments had failed. A line connecting them—wide, swooping, intersecting in one perfect curve.

"This isn't a theory," he said softly.

"It's architecture."

The warm wind didn't stop.

Even as they entered temperate latitudes, it stayed with them—curling around the rigging, rising from the bilge. The barometers registered stable pressure, but the crew felt squeezed. As if the ship sailed not through air but a tunnel of unseen mass. Compass drift returned.

Stars flickered in strange rhythms.

At night, the auroras came again—far too south for that time of year, veils of green and red undulating across the sky. The scientists debated sunspot activity. Magnetic flux. Atmospheric anomalies.

But none could explain why the auroras pulsed *in rhythm* with

Hartley's breath.
The humming got louder.

They reached Auckland under silence.

The ships needed repair.

The men needed shore leave.

But no one disembarked with joy.

The fleet pulled into harbor like a funeral procession. Officers walked stiffly. Sailors drank too fast. The naturalists refused to open their boxes. Wilkes delivered a brief statement to the governor—nothing beyond "survey completed, proceeding with mission."

He was back aboard before sunset.

That night, the sea glowed.

Not the whole ocean—just the patch beneath the *Peacock*.

Pale blue.

Like bioluminescence, but slower. Thicker. It didn't pulse like plankton.

It *flowed* upward.

And every man on deck saw it.

And said nothing.

The next morning, Hartley spoke.

Not in English.
Not in any known language.

He sat upright in his cot, eyes still closed, and began reciting a string of syllables that made the rigging vibrate. The doctor froze. The steward ran. Wilkes was called.

By the time he arrived, Hartley had gone silent.

But the metal basin beside the bed—where they kept the wash-water—was vibrating so violently it shattered.

No one touched it.

They just watched the water spill across the floor and slide toward the hull.

Wilkes convened a private meeting with his senior officers.

No logs were kept.

No transcript exists.

But afterward, the mission changed.

They would not proceed west as planned.

They would head back to the southern ocean.

Just once more.

Just close enough.

Just to *confirm*.

He said it calmly.

But his hands trembled.
The others nodded.

Not because they agreed.

But because no one wanted to be the one to say no.

And so they turned.

One more time.

Back toward the place the world didn't want charted.
Back toward the silence.
The warmth.

The spiral beneath the sea.

They called it "Course Echo."

A route that didn't exist on any chart, plotted by hand from

Wilkes' personal notes and compass-corrected calculations. It curved like no sane sea path should—not from port to port, but from *event* to *event*. It passed through anomalies. Heat zones. Places where stars shifted, where compasses stalled, where the sea pulsed without tide.

They didn't tell the crew.

They just sailed.

The *Peacock* took point, followed by the *Flying Fish* and the *Porpoise*. The other vessels were ordered to proceed on official survey missions. Only the chosen three would make the detour. The rest were given sealed packets.
In case they didn't return.

The warm wind grew stronger.

Now it wasn't just a current—it was a force.

It pressed against the sails even in still air. It curled into sleeping quarters. It made metal hum. The ship's dog—an old terrier kept for ratting—refused to go below deck. It sat at the bow, eyes fixed on the sea, teeth bared at nothing.

Men began hearing voices again.

Not dreams now.

Waking.

The boatswain of the *Flying Fish* was found speaking to the ship's hull, repeating the word "welcome" over and over.

He was restrained.

And kept under watch.

But the others heard it, too.

A voice in the wind, not loud, not distinct, but *present*. Like breath against the ear. Not angry.

Just aware.

On the sixth day of Course Echo, the water turned glassy.

No waves.

No ripples.

The sky a pale sheet of silver.

No birds.

No clouds.

Then, beneath the *Peacock*, the water *parted*.
Not a whirlpool.
Not a vortex.

It *opened*, gently, as if exhaling.

And for a moment, they saw it.
A circular depression in the ocean, smooth and vast, descending in perfect symmetry.
A spiral.

Down.
Down.
Down.

Wilkes ordered no entry.

No boat lowered.
No approach.

They sailed around it.

Measured.

Recorded.

And left.

But no one spoke for hours.

They simply drifted on.

Each man facing forward.

Each man knowing they had seen something that wasn't supposed to be seen.

Hartley was gone the next morning.

Not dead.

Not missing.

Just *gone*.

His cot was empty.

His sheets were folded.

His boots placed neatly by the door.

There was no splash.

No signs of struggle.

Just one message, scrawled on the wall in ash:

"It opens to those who hear."

Wilkes had it scrubbed clean.

But the men remembered.

Because every one of them had heard something.

That night, the aurora returned.

But not in the sky.
In the water.

Waves of light beneath the surface—green, violet, deep crimson—like something vast was turning beneath them. The temperature rose again. The decks steamed. The sails glowed faintly.

And from the depths, the sound returned.

Not humming now.

Calling.

Low. Vibrating. Almost *joyful.*

As though whatever was down there knew they had come close.

And approved.

The next day, Wilkes changed course again.
Back north.

No explanation.

No orders.

He simply stared at the sea and whispered, "That's enough."

And for once, no one questioned him.
They turned the bow toward home.

But the wind didn't follow.

It *led.*

Pushing them northward.

Guiding them.

As if the Earth itself had acknowledged them.
Tagged them.

Marked them for something yet to come.

In the final log of the *Peacock* before the expedition made port, a young ensign wrote:

"We did not map the unknown. We shook its hand."

And as the ships vanished over the curve of the horizon, the spiral beneath the sea continued to turn.

Slowly.

Patiently.

As if waiting for the next voice brave—or foolish—enough to answer.

Chapter 9: Mutiny and Madness – When the World Turned Inward

It didn't happen all at once.

It never does.

First it was little things. Missed orders. Incorrect readings. A logbook left open, then missing entirely. Then the men began isolating themselves—choosing to eat alone, refusing to sleep below deck, walking the length of the ship at odd hours. Some stopped speaking altogether. Others wouldn't *stop*, mumbling constantly about depth, about wind, about things "seen from the corner of the eye."

Then came the scratching.

Not rats.

Men.

Etching spirals into their bunks. Into the decks. Into their skin.

It spread from the *Peacock* to the *Porpoise*. Then to the *Flying Fish*.

Within two weeks of leaving Course Echo, the fleet was quietly unraveling.

And no one dared say why.

Wilkes tried to reassert order. More drills. More discipline. He doubled the watch schedule. Assigned new tasks to distract the worst cases. But the damage had been done. Not physical. Not even mental.

It was *spiritual.*

They had looked into the dark place beneath the world.
And something had looked back.

The officers held tight for longer than the crew.
But even among them, fractures formed.

The cartographer of the *Flying Fish* burned every map from the
southern leg of the expedition. Said the lines were "wrong,"
that the angles had changed. When restrained, he screamed for
five hours straight—until his throat collapsed.

He died two days later.

His final words: *"There's more world beneath the world."*

On the *Peacock*, the naturalists sealed their specimens and refused to open them. One threw a crate of preserved sea slugs
overboard. Another set fire to his own field journals, saying he
wouldn't "bring that shape back to civilization."

Wilkes confronted him.

The man only pointed to the smoke and said:

"It's inside the ink."

By the time they reached Honolulu, the word "mutiny" had
begun circulating—not in shouts, but in silence. A shared understanding among the men that something had to *break.*
They had touched madness.

Now they wanted to hand it back.

The tipping point came when a midshipman struck his commanding officer during a drill. No provocation. No hesitation.

Just a blow across the face and the word *"No."*
He was chained in the hold.

But that night, two sailors released him.

They didn't run.

They just stood on deck, waiting.

And when Wilkes arrived, they said only this:

"We're not going back. You hear it. We know you do."

Wilkes didn't reply.

He turned.

And ordered the guns loaded.

There was no full mutiny.

There was no battle.

Just a slow, quiet defection of the soul.

The men didn't rise up.

They *sank*.

One by one, retreating into themselves, following some inner spiral back toward the silence they'd met below the ice.

By the time they left Hawaii, five sailors had gone overboard. Voluntarily.

Their clothes left neatly folded.
No splashes heard.
Just absence.

Hartley was still gone.

His name remained on the muster roll.
But no one could remember what he looked like anymore.

Even Wilkes avoided the question.

He had stopped writing in his journal.

He had started drawing instead.
Spirals.

Endless spirals.

Like drills.

Like tunnels.

Like doors.

And in the lower decks of the *Peacock*, the humming had re
turned.

But it wasn't coming from the hull.
It was coming from the *men*.

Their chests resonating with something they couldn't name.

They didn't speak of Hollow Earth.

They didn't need to.

It was *inside* now.

The madness had already begun.

They arrived in San Francisco with half the fleet listing and a silence thicker than fog.

Officially, the U.S. Exploring Expedition had completed its circuit. Four years, six ships, eleven thousand miles. They had charted the Pacific, surveyed Antarctica, brought back hundreds of new species, and filled entire crates with data. The Navy would call it a triumph.

But the men knew better.

The real voyage hadn't been mapped in degrees and latitudes. It had happened *beneath* the expedition.

And it wasn't over.

Wilkes was the first to land, stepping onto the dock with the gait of a man returning from war—not with victory, but with something *left behind*. His uniform was pressed, his expression unreadable. But his eyes scanned the horizon like a hunted man.

He refused all interviews.

Refused all questions.

Within a week, he had hand-delivered a sealed trunk to Washington. Contents: classified.

He was never questioned about it.

But he never sailed again.

The crew was scattered. Many were discharged immediately. Others were placed on leave. A few were hospitalized for "exhaustion," "heat delirium," or "unspecified neurological disturbances." One officer disappeared entirely—last seen walking toward the cliffs outside Monterey, a notebook under one arm.

When it was found, the only word inside—on every page—was:

Down.

The artifacts caused the most trouble.

Not the bones, shells, or preserved specimens—those were fine. The trouble was with the things they couldn't classify. The stone from the French captain.

The sealed sample from Temotu that registered an interior temperature of 98 degrees, even in a cold room.

The sketches of spiral patterns found beneath the ice.

No one wanted them.

The Smithsonian declined.

The Naval Observatory refused custody.

Eventually, they were stored in a government warehouse in Virginia, in a locked vault marked "Deep Archives."

Some say they're still there.

Others say the vault is empty.

But everyone agrees it hums.

Meanwhile, the story changed.

In the official reports, Antarctica was logged as "a region of extreme hostility." No mention of warm water. No mention of the fissure. Hartley was listed as "lost at sea." No one challenged it.

Reynolds was never mentioned.

Symmes' name was struck from the congressional records related to the voyage.

The words "Hollow Earth" were never written.

Not once.

But among the crew, the phrase became a code.

A whisper passed between men who woke sweating at night.

A way to say: *We know what we saw.*

And: *We're not the same.*

One year after the return, the chaplain from the *Flying Fish* hanged himself in the bell tower of his church in New Haven. His final sermon had been strange. Rushed. Disjointed.

He spoke of doors that should stay shut.

Of men swallowed by light.

Of gods that weren't gods at all—but watchers, waiting for the ground to crack.

He ended with a quote no one recognized:
"When the Earth breathes, do not inhale."

No one ever found the source.

Wilkes went quiet.

He retired early. Spent his days cataloging maps, writing papers, refusing all invitations to speak publicly. When asked in confidence what the expedition had truly discovered, he reportedly replied:

"The border of reason."

He died in 1877.

The stone on his grave reads simply:

Lieutenant Charles Wilkes
Explorer, Cartographer, Patriot

No mention of Antarctica.

No mention of the spiral.

But on the backside of the headstone, nearly invisible unless the light is just right, there's an etching.

A perfect, downward arc.

Half of a circle.

Leading somewhere you cannot see.

And what of the others?

Some became drifters.

Some were institutionalized.

A few wrote books—obscure, half-mad treatises on geology, mythology, and "psychic architecture." None were published in their lifetimes.

But all described the same shape.

A spiral.

Always the spiral.

Today, the maps are clean.

The Southern Ocean is cold, hostile, barren.

But if you know where to look—if you chart the logs, trace the routes, follow the whispers—you'll find it.

The warm current.

The pressure shift.

The sound.
Still there.

Still waiting.

The Earth has not forgotten them.
And it never will.

Chapter 10: Return and Redaction – What Was Buried

They returned as ghosts in dress blues.

The ships docked in New York Harbor under gray skies, greeted by trumpets and fanfare that rang hollow against the wet stone of the docks. Flags waved. Crowds gathered. Dignitaries read from prepared statements about "scientific progress" and "American courage." But the sailors didn't cheer. They stood at attention with hollow eyes and weathered skin, their faces unreadable, their thoughts somewhere below sea level.

The speeches meant nothing.

Because what they'd brought back couldn't be paraded.

It had no weight.

No name.

Only memory.

And it was heavy enough to sink a fleet.

Wilkes stepped onto land with the bearing of a man who'd won a war—but only barely. His uniform was immaculate.

His boots were polished. But his hands shook when he accepted the ceremonial sword from the Secretary of the Navy.

He did not smile.

He did not speak.

He saluted the crowd, then turned away.

It was over.

Or it *should* have been.

The data was transferred to Washington in locked trunks.

Specimens. Charts. Journals. Dozens of crates stamped with serial numbers and sealed with wax. Everything was inventoried, cataloged, and processed through the Naval Department's Bureau of Charts and Instruments.

But not everything made it into the official record.

Some boxes were routed to a secure location in the Capitol basement.

Others vanished en route.

One shipment, containing Hartley's cot, his clothing, and a satchel of personal notes, was "lost in transport."

The steamer carrying it was found floating adrift in the Chesapeake Bay, its cargo hold empty.

No crew aboard.

No damage to the ship.

The entry in the manifest was crossed out.
No explanation given.

A congressional review board was convened in 1843 to assess the results of the expedition. They expected maps. Taxonomy. Geological samples. What they received was...weirder.

Magnetic anomalies with no geographic cause.

Reports of spontaneous heat signatures in cold water zones.

Sketches of caverns "not consistent with known glacial formation."

One entry described "luminous fog that does not reflect light, but emits it."

The committee laughed.
Wilkes did not.

The final report was edited heavily.

Of the original 82 volumes of scientific data and journals compiled by the expedition, only 19 were published.

The rest were marked as "under review."

They were never released.

Today, they are considered lost.

But some say copies exist—in private collections, university basements, locked cabinets in the archives of the Library of Congress.

Not digitized.

Not scanned.

Only whispered about.

One document, titled simply *"Thermal Spiral Study—Wilkes Compartment,"* was reportedly requested for Freedom of Information Act release in 1996.

The request was denied.

No such file existed.
Officially.

Meanwhile, the public was fed a cleaner narrative.

Wilkes was named a hero.

The Ex. Ex. became the first great scientific voyage of the United States.

The maps were displayed.

The shells catalogued.

The Antarctic discovery—yes, land under the ice—was confirmed.

But the rest?

Redacted.

Hartley's name was struck from the final crew lists.

The sealed orders were never acknowledged.
And not one word was printed about the chamber.

Or the spiral.
Or the sound.

The sailors tried to go home.
Some did.
For a time.

But they didn't stay.

One by one, they disappeared from the record. They left behind wives, farms, debts. Some were reported drowned. Others simply...vanished. Letters stopped. Graves remained unfilled.

A few of the officers—those who could write—left behind accounts.

Fictionalized. Disguised.

But always the same core:

The world is not what it seems.

And we've been looking in the wrong direction.

One account—unsigned, but written in the same hand as Wilkes' journals—was found in the binding of a chart book recovered from a naval warehouse in Norfolk in 1922.

It reads:

"We were told to find land. We found something else. And once you hear it, you don't go back. You just go forward, downward, inward. Until you're part of the hum yourself."

It was never entered into evidence.

Just filed.

And forgotten.
Like the rest.

They burned the uniforms.

Not officially, of course. There were ceremonies, medals, reports filed in triplicate. But many of the crew who made it home took their Navy coats into barns, sheds, fields behind the house—anywhere fire would take—and set them alight.

It wasn't superstition.

It was containment.
They'd brought something back with them.

And they needed it gone.

The Navy never commented. No reprimands were issued. Perhaps because they knew. Perhaps because they had ashes of their own to sweep under the rug.

Wilkes vanished from public life within a year. He declined every invitation to speak. He ignored letters. When approached by journalists, he stared through them.

Neighbors said he walked at night. Always east, always toward the sea. Sometimes barefoot, even in winter. Sometimes humming.

No one could place the tune.

When he died, the medical report cited heart failure.

But the coroner made a note in the margin:

"Skin unusually warm."

The published accounts of the expedition became bestsellers.

Bound in gold leaf, stacked in libraries, passed through lecture halls. They were clean, heroic, scientific. Nothing supernatural.

Nothing strange. Antarctica was presented as an obstacle overcome. A triumph of American will.

But the men who'd stood on the ice knew better.

They didn't write their stories.

They lived with them.

Or tried to.

One settled in New Bedford. He opened a dry goods shop, raised three daughters, and drank himself to death before his fortieth birthday. He never spoke of the voyage. But on the night he died, his wife found a set of symbols carved into the floor beneath their bed.

Spirals.

Etched deep.

Scratched with something *hot.*

The floorboards had scorched edges.

They were never replaced.

Another turned up in Buenos Aires, leading a group of spiritualists. He claimed to channel messages from beneath the world. Said the Earth was hollow, yes—but not empty.

He said it was *alive.*

He published a pamphlet.

No one took it seriously.

But when he died, his followers buried him in a sealed chamber beneath the city.

The stone door bore a single word:
Below.

Back in Washington, the remaining officers kept their silence.

Some out of fear.
Some out of loyalty.

Some because they'd learned the cost of remembering.

One tried to blow the whistle—an assistant naturalist named Fenwick. He compiled a dossier of irregularities, including journal excerpts, unofficial temperature logs, and magnetic data that showed complete field reversal in three separate sectors.

He mailed it to three newspapers.

None of them published it.

Within a month, Fenwick was dead.

Riding accident, they said.
But his horse was found tethered to a tree half a mile from the cliff where his body was discovered.

The Navy moved on.

New missions. New ships. A war with Mexico. Then civil war.

The Ex. Ex. faded into history.

But not completely.

Because every few decades, someone would find something.

A forgotten box in a basement.

A map with annotations that didn't match any known code.

A stone sample still warm to the touch, ninety years later.

They'd ask questions.

And someone in a quiet suit would appear.

Not with answers.

But with an offer:

"We'll take that. It's part of an old case. Forgotten science. Nothing to worry about."

And then it would be gone.

In 1942, a naval researcher reviewing 19th-century expedition archives flagged a phrase in a handwritten journal fragment:

"The wind below is not weather."

He noted it.
Filed a report.

Three weeks later, he was reassigned.

To Antarctica.

He never returned.

The redacted material remains under lock and key.

Hundreds of crates marked "U.S. Exploring Expedition – Supplementary" sit in a secure facility under a false name. There is no record of who oversees them. They are not digitized. They are not loaned.

And yet, every year, one file is checked out.
No one knows by whom.

Or why.

The final entry in the unofficial captain's log, now lost, was said to read:

"They asked us to draw the line at the bottom of the map.
We did.
And then we stepped over it."

That line?

Still there.
Drawn in ink.
Buried in ice.

And vibrating.

Chapter 11: Science and Speculation – The Theory that Refused to Die

It should have ended there.

A strange man dies. A strange voyage is filed. Crates sealed.

Journals forgotten. The spiral quiet.

But the world doesn't forget that easily. It *stores* things. In dreams. In whispers. In margins. And sometimes, in fiction.

That's where the Hollow Earth went next.
Into stories.

The 1850s brought a different kind of explorer: the philosopher, the novelist, the madman with a pen. They didn't need ships. They needed paper. Ink. An audience.

The Earth was no longer just something to map.

It was something to imagine.
And what lay beneath it… was fair game.

The first to crack the door again was a man named John Cleves Symmes III—son of the son of the man who started it all. He wasn't a scientist. He was a poet. And in 1854, he published a strange, fragmented work titled *The Breathing Globe*, a poetic reflection on "the inhaling poles of our living Earth." It was ignored. Mocked. Then, quietly, quoted.

The ideas began to creep back in.

Not in universities.

In dime novels.

In 1864, Jules Verne published *Journey to the Center of the Earth.*

It was fiction. Of course. A German professor descends through an Icelandic volcano to discover a vast subterranean world. There are prehistoric beasts. An inland sea. Storms beneath stone. It ends with a volcanic eruption and a triumphant return.

It was adventure.

It was absurd.
But it was *based*—loosely, unmistakably—on earlier claims.

The names were changed.

But the spiral was the same.

Scientists scoffed.

They were busy now with real discoveries—Darwin, thermodynamics, electromagnetism.

But they missed something.

The Hollow Earth didn't need to be true.

It needed to be *plausible.*

That was enough.

Enough to haunt the footnotes.
Enough to inspire new versions.
Enough to survive.

The 19th century was the age of geology. Of deep time. The idea of a molten, shifting Earth took hold. Volcanoes. Plate tectonics. Core pressure. Heat. Pressure. Layers. Every new theory closed the door a little tighter on Symmes' dream.

But never all the way.

Because now and then, the anomalies returned.

Reports of unusual heat signatures in the Arctic.

Compasses drifting without magnetic cause.

Migratory birds flying north in winter—then never returning.

And always, in the background, the spiral.

Drawn on cave walls.

Etched on ancient tools.

Carved into stones that predated history.

Coincidence.

But hard to ignore.

In 1895, a Swedish engineer named Olaf Jansen claimed to have sailed *into* the North Pole.

Not over it.

Into it.

He told of an inner world, lush and temperate, ruled by beings twelve feet tall. He published his tale in a self-financed booklet called *The Smoky God*.
No one believed him.
Except a few.
And that was all it took.

The theory adapted.
Split.

Some said the Hollow Earth was a refuge—home to Atlanteans, Lemurians, lost civilizations. Others said it was the prison of the Nephilim, fallen angels exiled beneath the crust.

Some said it was an Eden.

Some said it was Hell.

By the early 20th century, it was no longer science or satire.
It was *myth*.

And myth, unlike theory, never dies.

By 1910, the U.S. government had quietly banned further civilian exploration near certain polar coordinates.

No explanation was given.

Just red zones on internal maps.
The reason?

"Geothermal instability."

But those who'd read the old journals—the ones never published—suspected something else.

A hum.

A pulse.
A memory.

The spiral reappeared in new places.

Etched into the bindings of books.

Stitched into the borders of flags.

Printed on the inside cover of a novel no one remembered writing.

Not proof.
Just patterns.
Just questions.
Just enough to keep the door cracked open.

Waiting.

By the time the 20th century gained momentum, the Hollow Earth had split into two realities.

In one, it was a forgotten footnote, a discarded hypothesis buried beneath layers of hard geology and seismographic proof.

The Earth had a molten core, a mantle, a crust. There was no room for caverns, continents within continents, or lost empires spiraling through the rock.

In the other, it had never gone away.

It had just changed its clothes.

Now it walked through séances, disguised as secret knowledge.

It whispered through fringe lectures and occult tracts. It showed up in the margins of spiritualist newspapers, nestled between stories of ley lines and ancient astronauts.

And in both realities, no one talked about the *real* expedition anymore.

Not officially.
Not directly.

But traces of it lingered.

In 1926, an obscure publication known as *The Midnight Magnet* ran a story titled "The Map the Navy Forgot." It included a hand-drawn chart of Antarctica with a circular depression at its center, surrounded by concentric rings.

The article claimed the map had been "retraced from an original brought back by a sailor who had seen what men should not see."

No name was given.

The Navy denied everything.
The magazine folded the following year.

But copies of that map resurfaced in conspiracy circles for decades, annotated by hand, the rings linked to harmonic frequencies and prophetic dates.

In the 1930s, a physicist named Dr. Walther Kuehn published a theory in a Berlin journal suggesting the Earth's poles might exhibit "hypergeothermal inversions"—a polite way of saying *heat rising from places where there should only be cold.*

He was dismissed.

His paper withdrawn.

But before his death, he added a note in the margin of his only surviving manuscript:

"The spiral is not a theory. It is a structure."

During World War II, the U.S. government reexamined old naval data from the Ex. Ex.

Not for Hollow Earth theories.

For strategic purposes.

Polar access.

Magnetic drift.

Fuel consumption at extreme latitudes.

But one file—a worn, water-stained report with no author— had a line that stood out:

"If approached again, entry must be either complete or never."

It wasn't signed.

It wasn't dated.

But the document was filed under "Legacy: Symmes."

The postwar years brought new lenses.

New cameras.
New aircraft.

And with them, new questions.

High-altitude flights over the Arctic reported visual distortions—auroral anomalies, compasses stalling, even aircraft instruments blinking out over certain latitudes.

All were dismissed as "aurora-related glitches."
But pilots told other stories.

One commercial flyer—never named publicly—claimed to have seen "a dark opening in the clouds beneath us, stretching down into the white, like a mouth."

He was reassigned.
He never flew again.

And then came the stories about Admiral Byrd.

A hero of polar exploration, Byrd had led multiple expeditions to both poles. In the 1940s, he returned from Antarctica with a face like stone and a silence too heavy for a man who had just completed a historic mission.

He spoke only in riddles.

He gave one interview.

When asked about the dangers of the poles, he replied:
"There are things more frightening than cold."

That was all.
But somewhere, deep in the National Archives, a logbook exists.

Stamped.

Redacted.

Unreadable.

And inside it, a single surviving phrase:

"Flight followed the spiral down."

No coordinates.

No conclusion.

Just the echo of something the Earth had tried once to share.

And what of Symmes?

Reynolds?

Wilkes?

Their names live on in street signs and historical footnotes. A monument in Ohio. A few dusty plaques. But their *story*—the true story—was swallowed.

Like everything else.
Into the spiral.

Today, Hollow Earth lives on in fiction, fantasy, cartoons, pulp novels. It's entertainment. A metaphor. A joke.

But some still look at the sky differently.

Some still notice when the wind comes from the wrong direction.

Some still hear the hum.

Not in the air.

In their ribs.
Their bones.
Their *memory*.
And they wonder…

If what lies below isn't fiction.

But a future waiting to be re-entered.
By those who remember.

And those who *never forgot*.

Chapter 12: The Occult Underground – When the Inner World Went Mystical

The scientists had rejected it. The Navy had redacted it. The historians had footnoted it out of relevance.

But the mystics?

They were just getting started.

While universities were diagramming the Earth's layers with cold precision, another world—beneath the lectures, behind the curtains—was rewriting the Hollow Earth not as a scientific possibility, but as a spiritual *truth*.

It began quietly, in drawing rooms and parlor salons. Candlelit gatherings in Boston, Brooklyn, Berlin. Mediums speaking in tongues. Crystal pendulums swinging in spirals. Whispered stories of tunnels beneath Tibet, of cities under the Sahara, of entrances hidden in symbols rather than snowdrifts.

They weren't looking for caverns.

They were looking for *portals*.

And they believed the Earth was not just hollow—

It was *sacred*.

By the late 19th century, theosophy had taken root—a sweeping spiritual movement that fused Eastern mysticism, Western esoterica, and the fragments of forgotten science. Helena Blavatsky, the movement's controversial matriarch, spoke of "hidden masters" living within the Earth, guiding humanity's evolution from a realm called *Agartha*.

It wasn't a metaphor.

Her followers believed Agartha was real—a luminous kingdom beneath the crust, shielded from the world's corruption, populated by beings of advanced wisdom and long-forgotten power.

They cited ancient Sanskrit texts.

They mapped underground cities.

And in the center of every diagram?

A spiral.

In London, a man named Edward Bulwer-Lytton published *The Coming Race*, a novel that blurred fiction and manifesto. It described a subterranean world inhabited by a superior race who wielded a force called *Vril*—an energy drawn from the Earth itself.

Edward Bulwe-Lytton

The book sold quietly.

But it ignited imaginations.

Vril became a buzzword in occult circles.

Soon, spiritualists were channeling Vril. Engineers tried to harness it. Secret societies formed around the idea that the Hollow Earth wasn't just a realm—it was the *battery* of all existence.

In New York, a faded copy of Reynolds' 1836 lecture resurfaced. Margins annotated in Latin. Lines underlined with peculiar symbols.

It found its way into the hands of the Hermetic Brotherhood of Luxor, an esoteric group that believed in reincarnation, astral travel, and subterranean enlightenment.

They republished the lecture in their private journal, inserting it into a cycle of sacred texts.

For them, Reynolds wasn't a dreamer.

He was a *messenger*.

They believed his ship never returned.

That it was taken.

Welcomed below.

Meanwhile, mountaineers in Tibet brought back tales of "shining tunnels" beneath the Himalayas. Shamans spoke of a realm called *Shambhala*—a paradise hidden inside the Earth, protected by silence and frequency.

In Peru, Quechua elders told of a serpent path leading down through the Andes into the "heart below."

In Iceland, the sagas whispered of *Ginnungagap*—not just the void between fire and ice, but the *place beneath the place*, where gods once walked.

Different names.
Same shape.
Same direction.
Downward.

By the turn of the 20th century, the Hollow Earth had become something new entirely.

Not a place to explore.

A place to *reach*.

Through meditation.

Through geometry.

Through blood.

Aleister Crowley, Britain's infamous occultist, referred to "the inner gate" in his journals. He never said where it was. Only that it could be opened, but only once. He warned:

"To descend is to dismember. To return is to forget."

He drew spirals obsessively in his margins.

He called them "soul circuits."

In France, Jules Bois claimed the Earth's core was "a rotating eye," and that its pupil could be seen only in states of trance. He described ancient civilizations—not lost beneath time, but *hidden* beneath terrain.

He was institutionalized in 1914.

His final written line:

"The hum is older than language."

None of this made headlines.

Not in the world above.

But below—in the labyrinth of secret societies, in the ink of hand-bound grimoires, in basements where chalk circles lit candles and seances fed silence—it flourished.

They believed the spiral was alive.

They believed it called to certain minds.

They believed the Ex. Ex. didn't fail.

It succeeded.
Too well.

And was buried, not because it found nothing…
…but because it found *too much.*

By the 1920s, the Hollow Earth no longer belonged to scientists, explorers, or even storytellers.

It belonged to the believers.

They didn't carry journals.

They carried talismans.

They didn't draw maps.

They drew sigils—spirals enclosed in runes, glyphs said to resonate with "inner harmonics." Some claimed to dream in frequencies. Others said they no longer dreamed at all. A few said they had *seen* it—Agartha, Shambhala, the City of Vril—never clearly, never twice the same, but always beneath. Always glowing.

And always humming.

New societies sprang up like fungi in the damp corners of the West.

The Inner Circle in Vienna.

The Vril Harmonium in Philadelphia.

The Polar Key Brotherhood in Buenos Aires.

They rarely published. They preferred whispers. But when they did release pamphlets, they read more like field guides for interdimensional spelunking than religious texts.

"Look for warmth where there should be none."

"The spiral descends through sound."

"When the compass lies, the gate draws near."

All of them referenced Antarctica.

All of them cited the 1838–42 expedition—though never by name.

They called it "the crossing."

Or "the descent."
Or, most cryptically, "the nod from below."

In 1933, a strange article appeared in *Les Cahiers Hermétiques*, a French occult periodical. It told the story of a man known only as "W," a former naval officer who claimed to have seen the gateway and lived.

He described a fissure in the ice, a room of light, and a "voice that vibrated through his bones."

He said the Earth was not hollow in the way we think.
It was *folded*.

He wrote:

"Beneath the crust is not space. It is reflection. The inside is the echo of the surface, dreaming."

The article was unsigned.

But the handwriting matched known samples from a surviving officer of the U.S. Exploring Expedition.

The periodical was seized by French authorities the following year.

In Germany, the Thule Society—an esoteric nationalist order—began mixing Hollow Earth lore with racial mythology, Nordic fables, and ancient polar mysticism. They believed

Agartha was not only real but the cradle of a superior race. They searched the world for entrances—Tibet, Greenland, and, eventually, Antarctica.

They weren't alone.

Others joined the search. Not for the sake of enlightenment.

For *power*.
The spiral, once a symbol of descent and return, was now seen as a source.
A machine.

A weapon.

But not everyone in the occult world agreed.

A schism formed.

Some—like the Theosophists—believed the Earth's inner realm was protective, benevolent, guiding humanity slowly toward evolution.

Others—like the Thule mystics—believed it was dormant strength, waiting to be claimed.

The disagreement wasn't academic.

It was spiritual war.

By 1939, secret expeditions had begun again.

Small teams. No press. No banners. Just ships, sleds, and silence.

They went south.

Few came back.

Those who did never spoke publicly.

But one researcher, a geologist's apprentice who abandoned his post in Argentina, left behind a single page in a field journal before disappearing from history:

"They called it paradise. But it watched like a god."

During World War II, Hollow Earth resurfaced in the strangest corners of intelligence chatter. Intercepts referencing "Operation Regenbogen" in the South Atlantic. U-boat sightings in ice fields with no documented exit routes. Claims that a base had been established beneath the ice "to wait out the turning of the world."

Officially, it was nonsense.

Unofficially, some files remain sealed.
And one fragment—declassified by accident in 1977—described a spiral-shaped heat signature under Queen Maud

Land, measuring nearly fifty miles in diameter.

The memo's header:

NAVINT SP/INFRA – Vibration Report
Status: "Inconclusive. Recurs every 48 hours."

Then the line:

"Frequency matches archived 1839 anomaly data."

No source listed.
No follow-up recorded.

Meanwhile, in backrooms and bookstores, the myth grew.

Comic books. Pulp novels. Radio serials.

The Hollow Earth was everywhere.

But it had changed faces again.

Now it was a world of monsters.

Dinosaurs. Mole men. Lost tribes with ray guns.
It had become safe.
Marketable.
A joke.

But beneath the absurdity, something survived.

In the symbols.
In the recurring shapes.
In the way people kept drawing spirals without knowing why.

One woman—a librarian in Spokane—reported receiving a package in 1952 containing a notebook bound in whale skin, filled with nothing but sketches of ice and concentric circles.

No note. No return address. Inside the back cover: a pressed feather, jet black, longer than any known species.
She burned the notebook.

But not before copying a single line that appeared between sketches:

"It breathes, even now."

The occult never let go.

Because they understood what the Navy had learned too late.
The Earth wasn't just a world.
It was a *mind*.

And like any mind…
…it could be opened.

If you knew how to listen.

Chapter 13: The Nazi Search for Agartha – Descent into Ice and Ideology

They didn't start with Antarctica.

They started with a myth.

Before the bombs, before the marches, before the swastika became a wound across the world, a small circle of German occultists gathered in candlelit libraries and Bavarian lodges, tracing a line from the Himalayas to the poles, from the lost city of Atlantis to the inner world beneath the ice.

They weren't scientists.

They were *seekers*.

And they believed the Earth was hollow.

Not as a theory.
As a *doctrine*.

The Thule Society had already taken root in Munich by 1919—equal parts mystical salon, nationalist breeding ground, and secret society obsessed with "Aryan origins." They devoured the works of Blavatsky, Bulwer-Lytton, and the Vril believers. They scoured Sanskrit texts for references to Shambhala and Agartha.

Their conclusion?

The master race did not come from the stars.

It came from *below*.

From an inner world—ancient, radiant, forgotten.
A world where light rose from the ground and gravity spiraled inward.
A world they intended to reclaim.

By the time the Nazis came to power, the Thule worldview had metastasized into the state itself. Heinrich Himmler, head of the SS and architect of the darkest corridors of Nazi ideology, became its high priest.

He wasn't just building a military.

He was building a mythology.

And at the center of it stood Agartha.

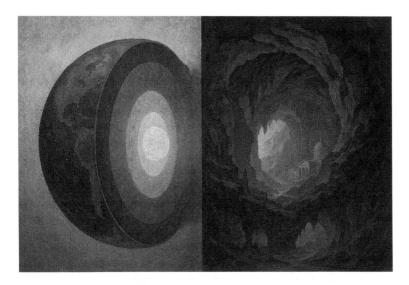

Himmler founded the *Ahnenerbe*—a state-sponsored research institute tasked with proving the superiority and sacred origins of the so-called Aryan race. On paper, the institute studied archaeology, history, linguistics.

In reality?

They chased ghosts.

They searched for Atlantis.

They excavated ancient Germanic temples for hidden codes.

They funded expeditions to Tibet, to Iceland, to the South Atlantic.

And always—quietly—they looked for *the entrance*.

In 1938, under the guise of scientific exploration, Germany launched the *Neuschwabenland Expedition*—a voyage to Antarctica with the icebreaker *Schwabenland*, a fleet of flying boats, and a crew of scientists, surveyors, and SS men.

Publicly, it was about whaling rights.

Privately, it was about *Agartha*.

They mapped over 600,000 square kilometers of the Queen Maud Land region.

Dropped metal rods marked with swastikas into the ice.

Photographed strange formations from the air—circular ridges, ice shelves with geometric symmetry, deep crevasses that radiated heat.

One pilot, in a sealed postwar interview, described seeing "a hole in the ice, vast and black, too perfect to be natural."
He was found dead two weeks later.

Gunshot to the chest.

Ruled a suicide.

The official report of the expedition was 379 pages long.

Only 23 were ever published.
The rest?

Archived.
Then lost.
No one knows who sealed them.
No one knows where they are now.

Rumors persist of a hidden base—*Base 211*—carved into the Antarctic rock. An underground facility powered by geothermal vents, shielded by the ice. Some say it housed German scientists until 1945. Others say it still exists.

But most agree: the entrance, if it ever existed, is buried beneath glacial shifts and decades of silence.

Yet the coordinates have never stopped circulating.

Passed between fringe researchers, conspiracy theorists, and intelligence reports filed under "unfounded."

But always the same numbers.

And always the same *spiral*.

After the war, Allied intelligence scoured the Ahnenerbe archives.

What they found defied logic.

Not just war crimes.

Not just pseudoscience.

But *maps*—detailed sketches of the Earth's interior as a series of concentric spheres. Flight charts showing polar entry points.

Energy diagrams labeled "Vril Gates." References to Reynolds.

To Symmes. To Wilkes.

And beneath it all…
…the humming spiral.

One OSS report, declassified in the 1980s, included this passage:

"It appears certain high-ranking Nazis believed contact with a subterranean intelligence was not only possible, but imminent. Several claimed the war would be won 'from within the Earth.'"

It was dismissed.

Filed under "Enemy psychological degradation."
But someone, somewhere, kept the file open.

Because the theory didn't die with the Reich.

It went underground.

Literally.

The war ended in ruins.

Berlin fell.

Bodies were buried.
Documents were burned.

But not *all*.

Because the idea of Agartha—the Hollow Earth, the secret entrance beneath Antarctica—wasn't just a curiosity of Nazi mysticism. It had become something far more insidious.

A *blueprint*.
A final contingency.

In the aftermath, Allied forces turned their attention south.

There were rumors—whispers passed between prisoners and picked up in decoded radio bursts. That high-ranking Nazis had fled not to Argentina, but *beyond*—into the ice. Into something *beneath* the ice.

Submarines unaccounted for.
Flight plans erased.
A place marked "211."
Nothing more.

Just a number. Just coordinates.
Just *enough*.

In 1947, just two years after the war, the United States launched **Operation Highjump**—officially, a massive military expedition to Antarctica, led by Rear Admiral Richard E. Byrd.

Thirteen ships.

4,700 men.

Planes, helicopters, survey crews, scientists.
It was one of the largest operations ever mounted in the Antarctic.

On paper, it was a training mission.
Unofficially?

It was a search.

The mission was scheduled for six months.

It ended after just eight weeks.

No reason given.

The press was told that conditions were too harsh. That fuel was low. That equipment had failed.

But among the crew, other stories circulated.

That planes had vanished.

That radio contact had been lost.

That *something* had been seen moving beneath the ice—faster than the wind, hotter than the sun.

One pilot described "a craft rising from the snow without sound."

Another claimed they saw a canyon where no canyon should exist—spiraled walls of ice, steam rising from below.

The logs of those missions?

Classified.
Still.

Admiral Byrd gave one interview upon returning.

A Chilean newspaper quoted him:

"The greatest threat may come from the polar regions."

When asked to elaborate, Byrd refused.
The quote was retracted days later.

Officially, he never said it.

But the rumor endured.

As did the silence.

Meanwhile, in South America, the Nazi diaspora swelled.

Colonies grew in Argentina, Paraguay, Chile.

Some claimed scientists from the Third Reich had brought with them blueprints for "inner world technologies." Subterranean craft.

Energy drawn from magnetic lattices.

A directional drill capable of tunneling not through rock, but through *resistance*—as if the Earth itself were a membrane.

The details were scarce.

But one thing appeared again and again in surviving documents:

The Spiral.

In 1951, a Brazilian newspaper printed a sensational headline: **"Nazi Remnants in Patagonia Seek Hollow Earth Return"**

The story claimed former SS officers were attempting to locate the original entrance described in Symmes' lectures, guided by

a mix of Reynolds' maps, Nazi engineering, and occult symbols.

The article was widely mocked.

Then retracted.
Then forgotten.
But the editor resigned.

And the reporter disappeared.

By the 1960s, Agartha had become something else.

A Cold War curiosity.
A footnote in intelligence briefings.

A "cultural phenomenon" noted by CIA analysts in fringe group behavior.

But someone, somewhere, still believed.

And in the vaults of postwar archives, pieces of the Nazi spiral resurfaced.

Blueprints for underground bases labeled *"Echo Rings."*
Antarctic maps with warm zones outlined in red.

A note in German, written in trembling script:

"They allowed us to see it. But not to enter."

No explanation.

No context.

But the spiral kept turning.

Today, some say Base 211 never existed.

That it was a cover for failed operations, a myth stitched from paranoia and desperation.

But others disagree.

Because the coordinates still appear.

In radio chatter.
In leaked intelligence.

In digital breadcrumbs left by people who disappear just after they post.

And in one satellite image—quietly scrubbed from government archives but preserved by amateur archivists—something remains.

A heat signature.
Near the pole.
In a perfect spiral.
Fifty miles wide.
Still pulsing.

It is not proof.

But it is not gone.
Because ideas don't die.

They *hibernate*.

And somewhere beneath the ice, beneath the politics, beneath the noise of history, the vision of Agartha still hums.

Not as fantasy.
As memory.
As warning.

Or invitation.

Chapter 14: Operation Highjump and Admiral Byrd – The War That Wasn't

They told the world it was training.

That Operation Highjump—thirteen ships, 4,700 men, dozens of aircraft—was a postwar readiness drill. A logistical exercise to test survival in extreme conditions. A peacetime flex in the most remote corner of the planet.

But you don't send a battle group to the bottom of the world for *practice*.

Not with destroyers.

Not with aircraft carriers.

Not with orders marked *sealed until return*.

Something else was happening in Antarctica.

And Admiral Richard E. Byrd, America's most decorated polar explorer, was at the center of it.

Admiral Byrd

The mission launched in December 1946.

The fleet—dubbed Task Force 68—set out with extraordinary resources: aircraft fitted with advanced surveillance equipment, scientific teams trained in geological survey, and a command structure that reported directly to the Chief of Naval Operations.

They arrived off the Antarctic coast in January 1947.

But from the moment they reached the ice, the story shifted.

Planes crashed under clear skies.

Radar flickered out.

Ships lost contact.

And the temperature readings made no sense.
One flight crew reported a thermal pocket 70 miles across—air temperatures 40 degrees warmer than the surrounding region.

Nothing in their training prepared them for that.

Nothing in *science* did either.

Byrd remained composed.

Publicly.

But in private communications—those declassified decades later—his tone darkened.

"Magnetic anomalies," he wrote, "beyond explanation."

"Light distortion near the southern ridge."

"Uncharted geological formations that appear engineered."

One message, never sent, was found in his personal diary:

"We are being observed."

No recipient.

No signature.

Just that single sentence.

Then came the flyover.

February 19, 1947.

Officially, it was a routine aerial survey.
But the logs were sealed.
Crewmen never spoke of it.

And Byrd—normally loquacious, even grandstanding—went silent.

What we know comes from fragments.

A recovered cockpit recording, partially transcribed, includes the following:

"Temperature rising... impossible... there's no snow here—Christ, that looks like..." [static]

And then:

"They're not... they're not hostile. They knew we'd come."

The tape ends there.

So does the official record.

Within days, Operation Highjump was over.

Six months of scheduled deployment terminated after just eight weeks.

No announcement.

No explanation.
The ships turned and left.
Fast.

Byrd flew to Washington.

Straight to the Pentagon.

No press conference.

No interviews.

Until one.

It was March 5, 1947.

The *El Mercurio* newspaper in Santiago, Chile, published a brief interview with Byrd. Translated, it read:

"Admiral Byrd declared today that it is imperative for the United States to initiate immediate defense measures against hostile aircraft originating from the polar regions. The Admiral stated that in the event of a new war, America could be attacked by flying objects which could travel from pole to pole at incredible speeds."

The quote was pulled within days.
The paper retracted it.

Byrd denied ever saying it.
But the story had already spread.

Back in Washington, a quiet storm brewed.
Reports were classified.
Debriefings redacted.

Medical logs—particularly psychiatric assessments—vanished.

One pilot, interviewed under oath, claimed they'd "seen a city made of ice that reflected no light." He later recanted. Then disappeared.

The head meteorologist on the mission filed for early retirement. His resignation letter read:

"The weather down there knew we were coming."

He never spoke publicly again.

What did they see?

A lost civilization?

A geothermal anomaly?
A mirage?
No official theory was ever released.

But unofficially, among intelligence circles, one word kept resurfacing:

Agartha.

The mission logs were eventually entered into the National Archives—heavily redacted. Pages missing. Coordinates blurred. But one fragment remains, tucked between equipment checklists and supply records:

"No entry permitted. No flight permitted. They will know if we return."

No context.
No author.
Just a directive.

Or a warning.

Admiral Byrd died in 1957.

He was buried with full honors.

A statue stands in his name.

But among the men who served with him on Operation Highjump, his legacy was something else entirely.

He had *seen* it.

He had been there.

And he had *left it alone.*

The rumors didn't stop when Byrd died.

They *multiplied.*

Because the expedition had left too many questions unanswered. Too many sealed reports. Too many conflicting accounts from men trained to be precise. The silence spoke louder than any press release.

And the spiral showed up again.

Not in maps this time.

In people.

One of the flight engineers, discharged in 1948, built a small shack outside Fairbanks, Alaska. He refused interviews. Refused visitors. But after his death, a journal was found in a locked drawer. The last pages were written in red ink.

"It's under us. Not down. Not below. UNDER."

"The ice breathes."

And finally:
"They knew our names."

He had never spoken of the expedition after returning.

But something had *followed* him home.

Then came the Byrd Diaries.

A document surfaced in the 1990s, passed hand-to-hand through UFO conferences and fringe forums. It claimed to be a transcript of a secret personal journal from Byrd himself—allegedly written after his February 1947 flight.
Most historians dismiss it as a forgery.

And yet...

In the supposed diary, Byrd describes descending through an opening in the Antarctic ice. Of entering a realm lit from within. Of seeing craft—silver, silent—rise from the snow. Of being greeted by tall beings who communicated telepathically and delivered a warning:

"Your world is not ready."

Byrd was escorted out. Returned to his plane. Told to deliver the message.

And stay away.

None of this is provable.

But none of it ever quite *goes away*, either.

Because satellite thermal scans—some leaked, some quietly published in academic corners—still show heat anomalies near the supposed coordinates of that flight. Because navigational instruments still go haywire in certain zones. Because modern

expeditions, despite having better technology than Byrd ever dreamed of, never go near those spots.
And because the spiral still hums beneath the ice.

The strangest thing?

Byrd never changed his story.

Or gave one at all.

After that quote in *El Mercurio*, he clammed up. He stopped speaking about Antarctica entirely. When asked about Operation Highjump in his later years, he would only say:

"We accomplished what we were meant to."

No elaboration.

No notes.

Just the look of a man who had flown farther than anyone expected—and turned back because he *had* to.

In 1956, a new Antarctic mission was launched—smaller, quieter.

Byrd was involved.

Barely.

He served as an advisor. Observed the planning.

But when the time came to fly south again, he declined.

His official reason: health.

Unofficially, his aide claimed Byrd stood at the window of the planning room, staring at a map of Queen Maud Land.

And whispered:

"That's where the silence begins."

After his death, his papers were reviewed by the Smithsonian.

Most were routine.

Maps. Flight logs. Letters.
But one box, marked "PRIVATE," was empty.

The inventory record notes it once contained "Geothermal flight reports – Operation HJ." Its file number: #1839-REY.

The catalog entry ends with one word.

"Withheld."

And so the spiral lives on.

Not just in the ice.

But in the minds of those who wonder.

Those who read the margins.

Those who still believe that Byrd found something.

Something not meant for conquest.

Not meant for science.

Just *meant to be known.*
Briefly.

Then forgotten.

Today, Antarctica is a land of treaties and taboos.

No mining.

No weapons.

No independent exploration without permits and escorts and eyes that watch every move.

The official reason?

Environmental preservation.
But some say the real reason is buried under the ice.

In that warm place where the winds don't blow.

Where compasses turn to nonsense.

And where the Earth, just maybe, opens.

Chapter 15: Theories in the Digital Age – The Spiral Goes Viral

It was always underground.

But now, it was *online*.

For over a century, Hollow Earth had lived in whispers—between the lines of redacted reports, beneath the chants of mystics, in the footnotes of forgotten expeditions. It survived in basements, in attics, in oilskin notebooks that smelled of mildew and salt.

But with the birth of the internet, the spiral didn't just resurface.

It *exploded*.

It began slowly.

Message boards in the mid-1990s—clunky forums with names like PolarGate, TheLastLayer, and EchoMap. Users shared scraps of lore: old newspaper clippings, scans of Byrd's supposed diary, magnetometer readings no one could trace. Most threads died quickly, swallowed by conspiracy clutter and alien lore.

But some threads grew.

And what they lacked in evidence, they made up for in *obsession*.

Then came YouTube.

In 2007, a blurry video surfaced titled **"Hole at the South Pole – NASA Cover-Up?"** It was shaky. Zoomed in on a satellite image showing a dark patch over Antarctica, ringed in clouds. The narrator—a voice modulated through static—claimed the image had been removed from Google Earth twice, then quietly restored with altered pixels.

The video was viewed five million times.

Then deleted.

Then reuploaded.
Over and over.

It still circulates.

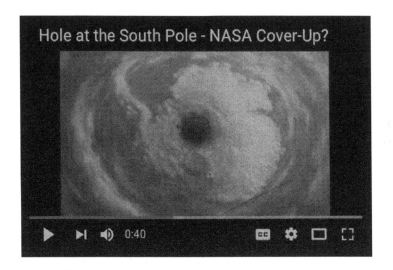

Reddit followed.

In subreddits like r/HollowEarth, r/ByrdWasRight, and r/DeepCartography, users built theories like cathedrals. They cross-referenced old naval records with declassified CIA files.

They built topographical overlays showing inconsistencies in Antarctic elevation maps. They tracked anomalies in migratory bird patterns. They even tried to 3D-model what a spiral-shaped thermal vent system might look like beneath the crust.

One user claimed to be the grandchild of a Highjump navigator.

Another claimed to have seen the original Symmes globe.

Neither could prove it.

But thousands believed them anyway.

Because now, the truth wasn't in documents.
It was in *volume*.
And the spiral spread faster than fire.

Memes helped.

A cartoon of a mole-man in Ray-Bans labeled "My neighbor Agarthan."

A doctored satellite image stamped with a spiral and the words "Exit   Only."

A gif loop of Admiral Byrd slowly turning into a reptilian. Funny.

Absurd.

But embedded in each was a seed of something else.
A *dare*.

What if it wasn't a joke?

Podcasts emerged.

Dozens.

Hundreds.

Episodes with titles like:
- "The Antarctica You're Not Allowed to See"
- "Why Hitler Went South"
- "NASA's Spiral Smokescreen"
- "Symmes' Hole: The Original Rabbit Hole"

They interviewed fringe scientists, self-proclaimed whistle-blowers, even a man who said he'd been *inside*—who described a city of light, a sky that glowed from below, and "voices like whales singing in binary."

He was laughed off the show.

But the episode had over a million downloads.

TikTok took it to the next level.

Fast. Visual. Emotional.

A teenager pointing at a globe, explaining how Antarctica is really a lid. A time-lapse of aurora borealis footage synced to audio recordings of whale song and "Byrd's frequency." A stitched clip showing polar research scientists abruptly cutting off interviews when asked about warm air.

A hashtag began trending: **#OpenTheIce**

Most videos were nonsense.

But some…

Some included footage that defied easy dismissal.

A radar scan pulsing in concentric rings.

A seismic chart that looped on a perfect interval.

A comment from a verified glaciologist that read simply:

"This was never meant to be public."

It was deleted within an hour.
But not before it was screenshotted 3,000 times.

And beneath it all, the *sound*.

Always the sound.

Lo-fi producers sampled low-frequency rumble tracks from old Antarctic seismic readings. They layered it beneath trap beats and synth loops, calling it "Earthcore." It became background music for meditation, conspiracy videos, even dance tracks.

But the vibration…
…it did something.

Listeners reported nausea. Lucid dreams. A feeling of falling.

One user posted:

"I played this through my subwoofer and the basement wall cracked. Straight line. Spiral etched in plaster dust. I'm not kidding."

No one believed them.

Everyone saved the video.

The Hollow Earth had become something new.

Not a theory.
Not a secret.
A *movement*.

Not because it was provable.

Because it was *possible*.

And in a world where every surface had been mapped, every border defined, every mystery debunked and defanged, the idea of a *hidden place* beneath the world—untouched, unbroken, alive—

That wasn't terrifying anymore.
It was *hope*.

The scientists kept laughing.

They wrote articles. They posted corrections. They drew cross-sections of the Earth's crust on whiteboards and filmed themselves saying the same thing: "There is no Hollow Earth. There is no Agartha. There is no 'hole.' Just pressure, heat, and molten rock."

But the more they explained, the more people believed.

Because *truth* wasn't about facts anymore.

It was about *resonance*.

And the Hollow Earth resonated.

With the uncertain.

With the disillusioned.

With anyone who felt like the world had closed all its doors and nailed them shut.
The spiral promised there was *one more*.

In 2017, a whistleblower posted a classified document dump on a dark web server. Among the files—most of which were dismissed as forgeries—was a single-page memo from 1983 marked NAVINT/SUBGEO/ANT-4.

The document included three data points:
- Seismic pressure fluctuation patterns in Queen Maud Land, identical to those recorded in 1947.
- Thermal vent activity from beneath 3.4 km of ice, measured at 121°F.
- The phrase: *"Confirmed match to Echo Spiral."*

No context.

No explanation.

It spread like wildfire.

Not because it was verified.

But because it *matched the story*.

The one they'd all been telling each other.
For years.

Meanwhile, a new term emerged: **"Echo Spiral Syndrome."**

It was coined in a Reddit thread.

Described as a feeling of gravitational anxiety when looking at certain images—particularly top-down satellite views of the poles.

Symptoms included vertigo, tinnitus, hypnagogic memory flashes, and dreams of descending tunnels.

No doctors recognized it.

But thousands claimed to have it.

One user posted a full 3D model of a spiral-shaped borehole after dreaming it.

Another claimed their infant son, before learning to speak, began drawing inward circles in the frost on their car window.

Every morning.

The internet did what it always does.

It made memes.

And then it started believing.

Some tried to go there.

Private expeditions.
Crowdfunded journeys.

One man flew a solo drone over restricted coordinates before the signal cut off. He uploaded the last frame: a mist rising from a smooth curve in the ice. The file corrupted halfway through.

He never flew again.

One couple claimed to have reached "the outer shelf" of the spiral on snowmobile. Posted photos. Then deleted them. Friends say they left the country.

No one's heard from them since 2021.

Their last post?

"It's not an opening. It's an eye."

The world governments stayed quiet.

But quiet in the way that *knows*.

In 2020, Norway denied access to an international science delegation seeking to drill near the old Neuschwabenland coordinates. No reason given.

In 2022, a joint U.S.–New Zealand flight was rerouted mid-air away from its approved glacier approach.

And in 2023, leaked documents suggested new construction permits had been granted for "deep access weather research" at the McMurdo Ice Shelf.

But when journalists tried to follow up, the contractor listed didn't exist.

The story died.

But the comments didn't.

Back on the internet, Hollow Earth had entered the mainstream.

Hollywood toyed with it.

A blockbuster movie hinted at a glowing jungle beneath the poles.

A streaming series followed a fictionalized version of Admiral Byrd into the spiral.

Merchandise followed.

So did music videos.

And TikToks.

And podcasts.
And virtual tours of a world no one could prove—but everyone could imagine.

One website offered "personalized Agartha passports" for $19.95.

Another allowed users to input their birthdate and location to calculate "spiral resonance alignment."

Was it all a joke?

Yes.

Was it also real?

To the people participating?

Absolutely.

Because something had shifted.

Hollow Earth was no longer just a theory.
It was a *belief system*.

Not a religion.

But a *ritual*.

To believe in the spiral was to believe:
That not everything had been discovered.
That some doors were meant to stay shut.
That *some maps lie*.

And that the Earth, for all its cataloging and strip-mining and satellite surveillance, might still be keeping one last secret...

Warm.
Waiting.

Turning just beneath our feet.

In 2024, a new YouTube channel appeared.

No name.
No intro.

Just a single video.

An old film reel, spliced with digital code.
A voice—calm, distorted—reciting coordinates in a rhythm that matched Hartley's breathing pattern from the sealed naval logs.

The last frame read:
"We didn't dig this.

We were invited."

Then silence.
No follow-up.

The channel disappeared.
But someone saved it.

They always do.

Chapter 16: The Symmes Legacy – The Man, the Monument, the Memory

It sits quietly on a patch of grass in Hamilton, Ohio.

A stone monument.
Modest. Weathered.

Rising just a few feet from the soil it claims to defy.

At its base, a name:

John Cleves Symmes Jr.

Beneath that, a sentence carved with unwavering conviction:

"He Contended That The Earth Is Hollow."

And above it, the strange shape that defined his life:
A sphere, pierced at the top and bottom, wide circular holes cut through it—his Hollow Earth, rendered in stone.

Not a grave.
A *statement*.
A challenge.
A question.

Most visitors don't stay long.

They take a photo, raise an eyebrow, maybe Google the name. They read the plaque about how Symmes was a war hero, a frontier philosopher, a madman of magnetic ideas.

Few linger.
Fewer still understand.

But those who do… feel it.
Not reverence.
Recognition.

Because whether they admit it or not, they've heard the hum too.

Symmes was never a scholar.

Not in the traditional sense.
He wasn't a geologist, or a cartographer, or a mathematician.

He was a soldier.
A reader.

A man who stood still long enough on the edge of the known world to *wonder.*

And when he looked at the poles, he didn't see limits.

He saw *openings.*

He believed Earth was not a sphere, but a shell.

That it opened at the poles.

That within it lay concentric spheres—habitable, lit by internal light, perhaps even populated.

He wasn't joking.

He *meant* it.

In 1818, he printed his Circular No. 1:

"I declare the Earth is hollow, and habitable within; containing a number of solid concentric spheres, one within the other... I pledge my life in support of this truth."

He distributed hundreds.
Thousands.

He sent them to members of Congress, university presidents, foreign dignitaries. He offered to lead an expedition. He asked only for ships and men.

He received… silence.

And then laughter.

The newspapers called him insane.

Caricaturists sketched him falling into his own theories.

But he didn't stop.
He toured.

Lectured.
Built models of his theory from paper and brass.

And people came.
Not scientists.
Not elites.
People.

Farmers. Miners. Merchants.

Ordinary Americans, bruised by war and birth-panged by a young nation desperate to define itself, listened to a man who dared say:

"There is more."

He died poor.
Exhausted.
Unheard.

In 1829, at the age of 49, he collapsed from illness in his sleep.

His final papers were never published. His dream—to lead a government-sponsored expedition to the polar opening—died with him.

Or so they said.

But that wasn't quite true.
Because one man listened.

Jeremiah N. Reynolds.

A writer.

A visionary.

A better speaker than Symmes. A smoother politician. And a believer.

Reynolds took up the cause, repackaged it, and brought it to Washington. He convinced Congress. He lit a fire in the Navy.

And in 1838, when the U.S. Exploring Expedition launched, the fire hadn't gone out.

They didn't use Symmes' name.
But they carried his question.

They didn't fly a banner.

But they followed his map.

And what they found...
Would never be printed.

The Hollow Earth wasn't Symmes' alone.

He had dredged it from the deep currents of human myth—reframed, redressed, and re-nailed to the bulletin boards of the modern world.

But the idea was ancient.

And he had reminded it how to walk again.

Not with certainty.

But with *doubt*.

And in a world obsessed with answers, doubt was dangerous.
It still is.

Today, Symmes is remembered as a footnote.

A crank.
A curiosity of early American eccentricity.

But in Hamilton, Ohio, the monument remains.
Not defaced.

Not forgotten.
Just... *there*.

Watching.
Pointing.
Waiting.

Because the Earth hasn't stopped turning.

And the spiral hasn't stopped humming.

You can trace it in the lines of history.

Symmes dies in 1829.

The expedition sails in 1838.

Reynolds vanishes from the record.

And Wilkes returns with silence in his eyes and a spiral in his chest.

That line?
It's not broken.

It's *buried*.

Because the true legacy of John Cleves Symmes Jr. isn't a theory.

It's a *pattern*.

Of explorers looking where they're told not to.

Of ships sailing beyond maps.

Of governments reacting not with denial—but with *containment*.

The shape of the story has always been a circle.
But its motion?

Always *inward*.

Symmes wasn't the first.

He won't be the last.

But he was the one who said it out loud.

'Who risked his name, his rank, his fortune on the claim that the world beneath our feet was stranger than we dared imagine.

He didn't do it for fame.

Or for profit.
He did it because he believed it.
And he died still believing.

That belief spread.
Quietly.
Virally.

It skipped generations like a hidden gene.

Popped up in unexpected places.

A farmer in Iowa building concentric greenhouses "to honor the inner sun."

A child in Patagonia carving a spiral into driftwood with no idea why.

A retired Navy radio man in 1964 swearing he still hears Morse code coming up from under the Pacific shelf.

These aren't stories.
They're *symptoms*.

Of something deeper.
Older.
Persistent.

In 2001, a private expedition—a small team of researchers and cartographers—attempted to follow Symmes' original theoretical route to the South Pole. They didn't make it. Engine failure. A medical emergency. Glacial drift. Whatever the reason, they turned back.

But one of them, a geophysicist named Mallory, left a note on his website before shutting it down.
It read:

"Symmes was right about the opening. He was just wrong about the shape."

That was all.

The page went dark the next day.

What was the shape?
Not a hole.
Not a tunnel.
Not a crater or cave.

A *resonance.*

A place not defined by geology, but by *invitation.*

You don't dig into the Hollow Earth.
You *descend*, if it allows you.
If it's ready.
If *you* are.

Symmes didn't live to see the echo.

But the monument in Hamilton whispers louder every year.
Visitors leave tokens now.
Spirals drawn in chalk.

Coins arranged in circles.

A note once pinned under a rock:
"Still listening."

Another:

"See you soon."

No one knows who leaves them.
But someone does.
Every year.
Without fail.

Theories fade.

But symbols endure.

And the spiral is still moving.

Through headlines.

Through satellites.

Through subwoofers and server logs and sonar pings that return with answers no one ordered.

And if Symmes were alive today?

He wouldn't beg to be believed.
He wouldn't argue.
He would *point*.

And say:
"Ask the Earth yourself."

So we come full circle.

To the man with the globe in his hands.
To the monument that still stands.
To the hole that may never open unless we listen for it.

Because the Hollow Earth was never just about what lies beneath.

It was always about what lies *within*.

Curiosity.
Obsession.
Descent.

And the idea that even now, in a world mapped down to the inch, we still haven't hit bottom.

Not really.
Not yet.

Epilogue: Look Southward

It begins with heat.

Not much.

Just a bloom—measured by satellite as a thermal anomaly beneath the Antarctic ice shelf. It pulses every 48 hours. Precisely. Predictably. Like a beacon buried too deep to decipher.

Scientists say it's geothermal activity.

A subglacial lake, perhaps. Tectonic friction. A volcanic vent that hasn't been mapped.

But the pattern doesn't fit.
The pulse is regular.
Mechanical.

Deliberate.

And it's growing stronger.

In 2022, a Norwegian research team stationed near Queen Maud Land recorded harmonic tremors beneath the ice unlike any known glacial shift. The frequency matched one recorded in 1947 by Operation Highjump. Exactly. No deviation.

They filed a report.

The data vanished.

So did one of their sensors.

And the only written testimony—the station chief's final log—
contained just four words:
"We are not alone."

Across the world, strange things stir.
Migratory patterns of Arctic birds change direction.

Whales surface in places they've never been seen.

A Chinese satellite malfunctions while scanning Antarctic to-
pography.

It reports—before blacking out—a heat plume shaped like a
spiral.

No press release follows.
But someone is watching.

Because every few years, a plane flies low over the pole.

Unmarked.

Unaffiliated.

Just one pass.

And gone.

There are rumors.

That a new expedition is being formed.

Quietly. Carefully.

Not military.

Not civilian.

Something in-between.

Its members have no public roles.
Its mission has no name.

Its destination: the region once known as "Echo Spiral."

They're not saying what they expect to find.

But one of the documents, intercepted by a digital leak in early 2025, included a phrase from a long-forgotten file, buried since 1839:

"Approach with reverence. The Earth remembers."

People have begun asking again.
Searching again.
Not in books.

In the ice.
In the hum.
In the possibility.

Because something is waking.

And whether it's a gate or a grave, no one knows.

But it's there.

Beneath us.
Within us.

Winding slowly upward like breath through a sleeping lung.

So look southward.
Not for land.
Not for conquest.
Look for the spiral.
The hum.

The warmth where there should be none.
The question buried for centuries beneath laughter and denial
and silence.

Because if the Earth is hollow...
...it is not empty.

And something is listening.

Visions of Hollow Earth

Edger Rice Burroughs

Admiral Byrd's Diary

David Ike

Jules Verne

Bulwer-Lytton

Emerson

Blavatsky

Kabbalist Lore

Aj M'Heji

Neitlich

Appendix:

Timeline of Events:

Prehistory & Myth

- **c. 30,000 BCE–3,000 BCE – Prehistoric Spiral Symbolism**
  - Spiral motifs appear in Neolithic cave art across Europe, the Americas, and the Pacific—possibly signifying cyclical time, descent, or sacred geography.
- **c. 2,500 BCE – Ancient Mesopotamian Underworld**
  - Sumerians describe a vast underworld (Kur) in their myths—separate, structured, and populated—accessed through gates in the Earth.
- **c. 2,000 BCE – Egyptian Duat**
  - The Egyptian afterlife is envisioned as an underground realm of fire, rivers, and passageways—traveled beneath the Earth by Ra each night.
- **c. 1,000 BCE – Hebrew Sheol**
  - The earliest Biblical texts reference Sheol, a shadowy realm beneath the ground where all souls go—neither Heaven nor Hell.

Classical Antiquity

- **c. 800 BCE – Homer's Odyssey**
  - Odysseus descends into the underworld, suggesting a literal terrestrial gate to another realm.
- **c. 500 BCE – Greek Philosophy**
  - Pythagoras and Plato propose the idea of a central fire inside the Earth and subterranean realms; Plato's Atlantis myth hints at hidden knowledge buried in lost lands.
- **c. 100 CE – Roman Geographies**

- o Roman scholars and geographers note strange
- o magnetic behavior and polar mythologies brought back from northern expeditions.

Medieval & Renaissance Thought
- **c. 700–1300 CE – Medieval Hell and Dante's Inferno**
  - o Christian cosmology solidifies Hell as a physical place beneath the Earth, described most vividly in *Dante's Inferno* as a descending spiral into sin.
- **c. 1200–1500 CE – Templar and Monastic Esoterica**
  - o Cryptic references to underground realms begin appearing in Templar records and apocalyptic Christian writings, especially during the Crusades.

Age of Exploration & Enlightenment
- **1640s – Athanasius Kircher's Hollow Earth Illustration**
  - o Jesuit scholar Kircher draws one of the first internal diagrams of the Earth showing fire lakes, central sun, and connecting tunnels.
- **1692 – Edmond Halley's Hypothesis**
  - o The famed astronomer suggests the Earth consists of concentric spheres, inspired by magnetic anomalies.

Symmes Era & Early U.S. Exploration
- **1818 – John Cleves Symmes Jr. Publishes Circular No. 1**
  - o Declares the Earth is hollow and habitable inside; petitions Congress for an expedition.
- **1829 – Death of Symmes**
  - o His dream passes to Jeremiah Reynolds, who reshapes it into a more persuasive appeal.

- **1836 – Reynolds' Lecture Tour**
  - His famous lecture *"The Interior of the Earth"* builds public and political support.
- **1838–1842 – The U.S. Exploring Expedition (Ex. Ex.)**
  - Under Charles Wilkes, the expedition allegedly pursues a classified Hollow Earth mission beneath its scientific cover—culminating in contact with anomalies in Antarctica.

Post-Expedition Mysteries
- **1843–1860 – Redaction and Silence**
  - Most Ex. Ex. data is withheld. Reynolds disappears. Wilkes never speaks publicly again.
- **1864 – Jules Verne's *Journey to the Center of the Earth***
  - Fictionalizes the idea for mass audiences—revives popular interest in underground worlds.

Occult & Esoteric Period
- **1870s–1910s – Theosophy and Inner Earth Beings**
  - Helena Blavatsky introduces *Agartha* and *Shambhala*—spiritual cities inside the Earth.
- **1871 – Bulwer-Lytton's *The Coming Race***
  - Introduces the concept of *Vril*, an underground force wielded by a superior inner race.
- **1938 – Nazi Neuschwabenland Expedition**
  - German explorers allegedly search Antarctica for entrances to Hollow Earth, possibly establishing *Base 211*.

Cold War & Highjump
- **1947 – Operation Highjump**
  - Admiral Byrd leads a massive U.S. Antarctic expedition. Mission ends suddenly. Rumors swirl of contact with underground forces and unknown aircraft.

- **1957 – Death of Byrd**
  - o Byrd dies under mysterious circumstances. His alleged "lost diary" circulates among conspiracy circles.

Digital & Modern Era
- **1980s–1990s – Fringe Theories Go Public**
  - o Declassified Cold War documents and UFO lore merge Hollow Earth ideas with secret bases, Nazis, and alien civilizations.
- **2007 – Viral Satellite Images**
  - o YouTube and Reddit erupt with videos and theories of polar anomalies and hidden entrances.
- **2020s – Theories Go Mainstream**
  - o Hollow Earth becomes a meme, then a belief system. TikToks, podcasts, and viral documentaries keep the spiral spinning.
- **2022–Present – New Heat Pulses & Expeditions**
  - o Scientists detect repeating heat patterns under Antarctica. A classified multinational expedition is rumored to be forming.

Key Characters and Historical Figures

John Cleves Symmes Jr.
Former U.S. Army officer and originator of the modern Hollow Earth theory. In 1818, he published his famous Circular No. 1, proclaiming that the Earth was hollow with open poles and habitable inner spheres. Though ridiculed during his lifetime, his ideas influenced explorers, mystics, and conspiracy theorists for over two centuries. His monument in Hamilton, Ohio, remains a pilgrimage site for believers.

Jeremiah N. Reynolds
A gifted writer, lecturer, and explorer who inherited Symmes' vision and made it palatable to Congress and the public. Reynolds' oratory galvanized support for the U.S. Exploring Expedition and introduced the inner world concept into America's scientific ambitions. His influence quietly shaped the goals of the Ex. Ex.—though his own disappearance remains one of its enduring mysteries.

Lieutenant Charles Wilkes
Commander of the U.S. Exploring Expedition (1838–1842). A brilliant but volatile leader, Wilkes navigated the expedition through the Pacific and Antarctic, allegedly opening a sealed directive ordering him to investigate Hollow Earth anomalies. After the voyage, he never again discussed the true purpose of the mission and withdrew from public life.

Lieutenant Hartley *(fictionalized composite)*
A fictional officer aboard the *Peacock*, used in the narrative to represent those affected by the mysterious energies encountered near Antarctica. After contact with a strange chamber beneath the ice, Hartley lapses into a trance-like state, becoming a symbol of transformation and lost knowledge. His fate is never fully explained.

Admiral Richard E. Byrd
Famed American polar explorer and naval officer who led *Operation Highjump* in 1947. Though the mission was officially scientific, Byrd reportedly encountered "unusual phenomena" near the pole, including anomalous heat and unexplained aircraft. His death in 1957 and rumored secret diary have fueled decades of speculation about what he truly found.

Helena Blavatsky
Founder of the Theosophical Society and major figure in the occult revival of the late 19th century. Blavatsky wrote extensively about Agartha and the inner world, claiming it was inhabited by spiritual masters guiding humanity's evolution. Her mystical vision helped transition Hollow Earth from science fiction to spiritual doctrine.

Edward Bulwer-Lytton

British novelist and philosopher who published *The Coming Race* in 1871, introducing the world to the energy force *Vril* and an advanced subterranean civilization. His novel became foundational to the occult and proto-fascist reinterpretations of Hollow Earth. Some Nazi leaders took it as literal truth.

Heinrich Himmler – may his name be cursed
SS leader and key architect of the Nazi state's occult ideology. Through the *Ahnenerbe*, Himmler funded expeditions in search of Agartha and other ancient sources of Aryan mysticism. He was reportedly obsessed with underground entrances in Antarctica and Tibet.

Olaf Jansen *(semi-legendary)*
Swedish fisherman who, in 1908, claimed in *The Smoky God* to have sailed into the Hollow Earth through the North Pole and spent years among twelve-foot-tall beings. His story is widely dismissed as fiction, but it remains a favorite among modern Hollow Earth enthusiasts.

Rear Admiral Byrd's Flight Crew *(various/anonymous)*
Pilots and radio operators on the 1947 Highjump expedition.
Fragmented records and unofficial accounts suggest some of
these men witnessed anomalies in weather, light, and geography—though none ever publicly confirmed the rumors. Several reportedly suffered psychological effects or disappeared
from the record.

Modern Digital Believers *(composite group)*
Reddit moderators, podcasters, TikTok influencers, and self-
proclaimed "mapwatchers" who keep Hollow Earth lore alive
in the 21st century. Though often seen as fringe, their online
presence has elevated the theory from obscurity to meme to
modern myth. They are the inheritors of Symmes' spiral—
armed with smartphones instead of sextants.

Pop Culture Influenced by Hollow Earth

Books & Literature

1. **Journey to the Center of the Earth** (1864) – *Jules Verne*
   The seminal Hollow Earth novel. A professor and his companions descend into an Icelandic volcano and discover a subterranean world filled with prehistoric life.

2. **The Coming Race** (1871) – *Edward Bulwer-Lytton*
   Introduces the concept of *Vril*, a powerful energy force wielded by a superior subterranean race. Inspired both occultism and Nazi ideology.

3. **Tarzan at the Earth's Core** (1930) – *Edgar Rice Burroughs*
   Part of Burroughs' *Pellucidar* series, where Tarzan journeys into a lush inner world through the polar opening.

4. **At the Earth's Core** (1914) – *Edgar Rice Burroughs*
   The first Pellucidar novel, featuring dinosaurs, stone-age tribes, and a hidden sun inside the Earth.

5. **The Smoky God** (1908) – *Willis George Emerson (based on Olaf Jansen)*
   Purports to be a true account of a Norwegian fisherman who sailed into the inner world through the North Pole and met a race of giants.

6. **The Hollow Earth** (1990) – *Rudy Rucker*
   A postmodern take where Edgar Allan Poe journeys into a wild inner Earth filled with bizarre geometry and strange civilizations.

7. **Subterranean** (1999) – *James Rollins*
   A fast-paced techno-thriller where a team of scientists discovers a lost ecosystem and intelligent life beneath Antarctica.

Movies & TV

1. **Journey to the Center of the Earth** (1959, 2008) – *Film adaptations*
   Multiple film versions of Verne's novel, with the 2008 version starring Brendan Fraser adding modern VFX and action tropes.

2. **The Core** (2003)
   A sci-fi disaster movie where a team drills into the Earth's core to restart its rotation. Features giant subterranean geodes and unexplained phenomena.

3. **Godzilla vs. Kong** (2021)
   Heavily features a Hollow Earth ecosystem that's accessible through energy portals and houses the "origin of the Titans."

4. **Godzilla: King of the Monsters** (2019)
   References Hollow Earth as the lair system of the ancient titans. Contains a hidden city beneath the ocean floor.

5. **King Kong (2005)** – *Peter Jackson*
   Skull Island, with its lost-world terrain and prehistoric monsters, is a thematic cousin to Hollow Earth myths.

6. **Land of the Lost** (1974 & 2009)
   A TV show and later a film about a family trapped in a hidden dimension full of dinosaurs and ancient ruins.

7. **Ice Age: Dawn of the Dinosaurs** (2009)
   The characters fall into a secret underground world filled with dinosaurs and jungles beneath the ice—Hollow Earth for kids.

8. **Doctor Who – "Infernals" arc (1970)**
   Features parallel Earths and drilling into alternate dimensions through the Earth's core.

Toys, Games & Collectibles

1. **Masters of the Universe – Subternia**
   Part of the He-Man mythos, Subternia is a realm beneath Eternia's surface. Featured in toys and multiple animated series.

2. **G.I. Joe – Cobra La**
   The 1987 movie introduced Cobra-La, a secret underground civilization with organic technology and ancient knowledge.

3. **The Inhumanoids** (1986)
   A short-lived but cult-beloved toy line and animated series featuring monstrous creatures from beneath the Earth battling environmental scientists in power armor.

4.

5. **Godzilla and Kong Action Figures (Playmates, NECA, SH MonsterArts)**
   Many 2021–2023 figures include "Hollow Earth" variants or accessories—like gravity ships, tunnels, and glowing terrain bases.

6. **Minecraft – Deep Dark & Ancient Cities**
   The game's recent updates introduce vast

underground biomes with their own lore, treasure, and ancient structures—clearly Hollow Earth–inspired.

7. **Dungeons & Dragons – Underdark**
A subterranean realm of its own ecology, civilizations, and elder horrors—frequently used in campaigns as a vast inner world beneath the surface.

Why We Are Fascinated with Hollow Earth

It begins before science. Before writing. Before the first maps scratched onto stone. Humanity's earliest symbols—carved into caves and cliff faces—spiraled inward. Not upward to the heavens, not outward across the sea, but *down*. Into the dark. Into the Earth.

From prehistory to the digital age, the idea of a world beneath our world has never gone away. It simply *changed shape*—from myth to metaphor, from spiritual realm to speculative science, from pseudoscience to pop culture. The Hollow Earth has always been more than a theory. It is a *mirror*. One we lower into the soil, hoping to see something ancient and unshaken staring back.

The Cave and the Cradle

In myth, the Earth has always been alive. The Greeks gave it a name—*Gaia*. The Egyptians imagined the underworld (*Duat*) as a shadow-mirror of life, where the sun passed each night. For the Norse, Yggdrasil's roots descended into the realms of death, giants, and rebirth. In nearly every culture, *below* meant something more than burial.

It meant *origin*.

We are burrowing creatures by instinct. We seek shelter in earth, build homes with stone, dig for minerals, tunnel for fuel. The notion that something older and wiser lives beneath us is primal. An echo of the womb. A return to the place where life begins—in the dark, in the warm, in the hollow.

Science and the Spiral

When Enlightenment thinkers replaced myth with measurement, the Hollow Earth refused to vanish. It merely *adapted*. Halley's magnetic shells. Symmes' concentric spheres. Verne's volcanic pathways. Each idea tried to reconcile physical law with an irresistible intuition: that Earth, like man, might be hollow not by accident, but by *design*.

The 19th century gave birth to geology, and with it came crushing certainty. Molten cores. Pressure. Plates. But every theory that closed the door on Hollow Earth opened another—a crack in magnetism, a flaw in the field, an anomaly that didn't quite make sense. And when science failed to prove the myth, fiction stepped in.

Journey to the Center of the Earth. The Coming Race. Tarzan at the Earth's Core. These stories didn't just entertain—they *satisfied*. Because they gave readers a map of a world that still held secrets, one more layered and more dangerous than the surface could ever be.

Subterranean Temples and Nazi Shadows

In the 20th century, Hollow Earth became more than an idea. It became a *weapon*.

Theosophists saw it as sacred. Occultists saw it as prophecy.

And fascists—most terrifyingly—saw it as justification. If a master race lived beneath us, untouched by time and decay, then conquest was no longer colonization—it was *restoration*.
The spiral was perverted. Turned into a symbol of purity, of secret knowledge hoarded and weaponized. From Thule to Tibet, from Nazi Antarctica to postwar panic, Hollow Earth stopped being a theory and became an *ideology*.
And yet—even then—it endured.
Because beneath the lies and horrors, the longing remained: for a place unspoiled. A city of light. A gate to *begin again*.

Digital Descent

When the internet arrived, the Hollow Earth didn't fade.

It *thrived*.

It jumped from lecture halls and dusty paperbacks into YouTube videos, memes, podcasts, and TikToks. It became entertainment. Then belief. Then community.

In an age where satellites map every mountain and algorithms predict every step, Hollow Earth offers a strange hope: that something vast and undiscovered still exists. That beneath the noise, the truth waits in silence. That under our feet—beneath concrete, bedrock, and magma—there is still mystery.

Not aliens.
Not demons.
Not even dinosaurs.
Just *more*.
More space.
More story.
More possibility.

The Cultural Allure

So why are we fascinated with Hollow Earth?

Because it promises reversal.

In a world that rewards expansion, Hollow Earth rewards *inversion*. It tells us the real adventure isn't outward—it's *inward*. The monsters we fear? Inside us. The paradise we lost? Beneath us. The future? Spiraling backward, down a tunnel of forgotten memory into a realm where nothing is mapped, and everything is felt.

It's the final refusal to believe that the world is finished.

That we've seen it all.
That mystery is dead.
To believe in Hollow Earth is to believe in *depth*—of the world,
of the soul, of history itself.

And to whisper back to the darkness:

We're still listening.

Admiral Byrd and the Hollow Earth: Fact, Fiction, or Something in Between?

In the annals of polar exploration, Admiral Richard Evelyn Byrd stands as a towering figure. A decorated naval officer, aviation pioneer, and leader of multiple Antarctic expeditions, Byrd's achievements earned him a near-mythic status in 20th-century American history. Yet alongside his genuine accomplishments, a curious legend has persisted—a tale that Byrd, during his 1947 *Operation Highjump* expedition, flew into a massive hole at the South Pole and encountered a secret, advanced civilization beneath the Earth's surface.

Is there truth to this story? Or is it the product of Cold War paranoia, misinterpretation, and decades of mythologizing? The answer lies at the murky intersection of documented history, redacted military files, and our deep cultural craving for mystery.

The Historical Byrd

Born in 1888, Richard Byrd was no stranger to adventure. After a successful naval career, he rose to prominence as a polar aviator, claiming the first flight over the North Pole in 1926 (a claim later debated) and leading several scientific missions to Antarctica. His leadership of the 1939–41 *United States Antarctic Service Expedition* and the massive postwar *Operation Highjump* in 1946–47 marked some of the most ambitious explorations of the southern continent ever undertaken.

Operation Highjump involved 13 ships, 4,700 men, and a vast array of aircraft and scientific equipment. Its official purpose was to test military capabilities in cold weather and reinforce U.S. claims in Antarctica. The expedition ended suddenly after just eight weeks, fueling speculation that something unexpected had occurred.

Enter the legend.

The Diary that Wasn't

The core of the Hollow Earth claim comes from a document circulated widely on the internet in the late 20th century: *Admiral Byrd's Secret Diary*. This alleged account claims that Byrd flew over Antarctica on February 19, 1947, entered a lush, green area beneath the ice, and made contact with beings from an underground civilization. These beings supposedly issued a dire warning to humanity about the dangers of nuclear weapons and environmental destruction.

However, nearly every scholar, historian, and Byrd biographer rejects the diary as a fabrication. There is no official record of such a document in Byrd's archives, and the language used in the "diary" does not match Byrd's known writing style. The account appeared decades after Byrd's death and was never corroborated by any of his crew or expedition records.

That said, several anomalies from *Operation Highjump* have remained difficult to explain—and have kept the legend alive.

Anomalies and Absences

First, there's the unexpected early termination of *Operation Highjump*. The mission was scheduled to last six months but was concluded after just two. Official explanations cite harsh weather and logistical challenges. However, unofficial accounts have hinted at something more. Several personnel reportedly experienced psychological distress. Some aircraft were damaged or lost under unclear circumstances. At least one pilot spoke cryptically in a post-expedition interview of "unnatural" phenomena over the ice.

Adding to the mystery is Byrd's 1947 interview with *El Mercurio*, a Chilean newspaper. He is quoted as saying:
"The greatest threat may come from the polar regions. In case of a new war, America could be attacked by aircraft flying over one or both poles."

This quote, though widely repeated, was later walked back by U.S. officials and allegedly misrepresented. Yet for conspiracy theorists, it added fuel to the fire—suggesting Byrd had seen something at the poles worthy of concern.

Cultural Context and Cold War Paranoia

Why did Byrd become the focal point for Hollow Earth mythology?

Part of the answer lies in the Cold War atmosphere of secrecy, mistrust, and technological awe. In the 1940s and '50s, the U.S. government was conducting secret operations, nuclear testing, and intelligence programs—many of which would not come to light for decades. This bred a culture ripe for speculation and suspicion. The idea that a secret Antarctic base—be it Nazi, alien, or subterranean—existed just out of reach captured the public imagination.

This period also saw the rise of the UFO phenomenon, the Roswell incident, and the popularization of esoteric ideas via the Theosophical Society and fringe writers like Raymond Bernard, who published *The Hollow Earth* in 1964. Byrd, as a public hero and polar explorer, became the perfect protagonist for a myth that blended adventure, conspiracy, and cosmic mystery.

Scientific Consensus

Despite these lingering tales, the scientific consensus remains clear: the Earth is not hollow. Seismic readings, gravitational measurements, and geological modeling confirm that the planet is composed of a solid crust, a viscous mantle, and a molten outer core surrounding a solid inner core. There is no evidence—empirical or photographic—of vast inner cavities, entrances at the poles, or underground civilizations.

Moreover, the conditions beneath Antarctica are extreme.

While subglacial lakes like Lake Vostok exist, sealed beneath miles of ice, they do not point to anything resembling a Hollow Earth habitat. These are isolated, hostile environments—scientifically fascinating, but far from hospitable.
Yet, the absence of evidence has done little to deter belief.

Myth as Mirror

Why does the legend persist, even in the face of debunking?

Because the Hollow Earth myth functions not as science, but as *symbol*. It taps into archetypes that predate modern civilization—journeys into the underworld, lost utopias, and hidden knowledge. From Plato's Atlantis to Dante's Inferno to Verne's *Journey to the Center of the Earth*, the desire to find a world beneath our own is as old as storytelling itself.

In Byrd, we see the embodiment of this archetype: the explorer who goes beyond the known, who touches mystery, and who returns changed—or silent.

And in the Hollow Earth, we glimpse the ultimate refuge from modern life: a place unspoiled, self-contained, and eternal. It is Eden inverted. It is Heaven turned inward. And in an age of climate crisis and geopolitical instability, it offers a strange hope—that somewhere, beneath it all, something untouched still waits.

Conclusion: Between Fact and Fascination

So is Admiral Byrd's story true?

In the strictest historical sense—no. There is no credible evidence that Byrd discovered a hole at the South Pole, contacted a lost civilization, or witnessed anything supernatural. The diary is almost certainly a hoax. The anomalies surrounding *Operation Highjump* have plausible explanations grounded in the harsh realities of Antarctic exploration.

But in a broader cultural sense, Byrd's story is *true enough*.

It is true to our need for mystery. True to our suspicion of authority. True to our longing for meaning in a world that feels increasingly mapped, measured, and explained. And perhaps most of all, it is true to the idea that history is never fully written—and that beneath the ice, beneath the archives, and beneath our own disbelief, something may still lie waiting.

Not proof.

Not passage.
But *possibility*.

Teacher's Guide – Operation Middle Earth

About the Book

Operation Middle Earth blends real historical events with cinematic nonfiction storytelling to investigate one of the strangest footnotes in U.S. exploration history: a military expedition allegedly launched to discover whether the Earth is hollow.

Based on the real-life theories of John Cleves Symmes Jr., the book explores how fringe science, myth, and conspiracy have evolved from the Enlightenment to the digital age.

Through journal-style chapters, historical profiles, fictionalized first-person accounts, and vivid dramatizations, students will engage with primary documents, evaluate fact vs. speculation, and explore the cultural power of belief.

Learning Objectives

By the end of the unit, students will be able to:

- Analyze how myth and science intersect in historical and contemporary contexts.
- Trace the development of pseudoscientific ideas from antiquity to modern conspiracy culture.
- Evaluate narrative nonfiction as both a storytelling and historiographic tool.
- Compare the influence of real exploration (e.g., the U.S. Exploring Expedition) with fictional accounts in literature and media.
- Develop critical media literacy around how information is shared, censored, and mythologized in the digital age.

Suggested Curriculum Areas

- American History (19th Century Naval Expansion, Age of Exploration)

- Literature (Myth, Science Fiction, Narrative Nonfiction)
- Civics / Government (Propaganda, Secrecy, Public Trust)
- Media Literacy (Internet Conspiracies, Satire vs. Belief)
- STEM (Geography, Geology, Theories of Earth Structure)

Discussion Questions

1. **Historical Truth or Creative License?**
   How does the author use historical facts alongside speculation to craft a compelling narrative? Where do we draw the line between dramatization and misinformation?

2. **Why Hollow Earth?**
   What psychological or cultural needs might the Hollow Earth theory fulfill across different historical eras?

3. **Government and Secrecy**
   Why might governments suppress or redact certain information? How does that relate to public trust—and the rise of conspiracy theories?

4. **Admiral Byrd and Operation Highjump**
   Do you think the author presents a fair depiction of Byrd's mission? Why might it still fascinate people today?

5. **Digital Age Mythmaking**
   How does the internet breathe new life into old myths? How do memes, TikToks, and podcasts influence belief systems?

6. **The Spiral as Symbol**
   Why do you think the spiral recurs throughout the book? What does it represent metaphorically and culturally?

Suggested Activities
- **Timeline Mapping**
  Have students build a visual timeline of Hollow Earth references from ancient myth to modern internet culture. Include myths, books, historical expeditions, films, and memes.
- **Debate: "Was the Hollow Earth Expedition Real?"**
  Divide the class into two sides—one defending the expedition as a plausible cover for deeper missions, the other debunking it as myth. Use the text and outside sources.
- **Creative Writing: Found Document**
  Ask students to create a fictional "recovered" letter, memo, or logbook excerpt from someone who encountered the Hollow Earth. Encourage them to write in the tone of the book.
- **Media Literacy Case Study**
  Analyze a viral Hollow Earth video or conspiracy theory online. Students evaluate the rhetoric, sourcing, and emotional appeal.
- **Cross-Curriculum Collaboration**
  Pair with an Earth science unit on geology. Have students contrast real Earth structure with historical theories.

Assessment Ideas
- **Short Response Essay**
  "Why do myths like Hollow Earth endure even after they are scientifically disproven?"
- **Research Paper**
  Students trace the evolution of one fringe theory (e.g., Hollow Earth, Atlantis, Flat Earth) and its influence in media and culture.
-

- **Multimedia Project**
  Create a mock documentary trailer, digital zine, or
  podcast episode exploring one chapter of the book.

Supplementary Materials
- *Journey to the Center of the Earth* (Jules Verne)
- *The Coming Race* (Edward Bulwer-Lytton)
- Primary source letters from Admiral Byrd
- Excerpts from Symmes' Circular No. 1
- Declassified Operation Highjump memos
- Modern Reddit/TikTok posts tagged #HollowEarth

The Spiraling Shape by *They Might Be Giants*

From their 1997 album <u>Factory Showroom</u>

Down, down, down you go No way to stop As you fall, hear me call No, no, no Listen to this warning and Consider these Simple words of advice Stop, stop, stop

Fogging the view, cupping face to the window In darkness you make out a spiraling shape Putting all reason aside you exchange What you've got for a thing that's hypnotic and strange

The spiraling shape will make you go insane (Everyone wants to see that groovy thing) But everyone wants to see that groovy thing (Everyone wants to see that thing)

And nobody knows what it's really like But everyone says it's great And they heard it from the spiral in their eyes

This could lead to excellence Or serious injury Only one way to know Go, go, go Go ahead, wreck your life That might be good Who can say what's wrong or right? Nobody can

Put out your hands and you fall through the window And clawing at nothing you drop through the void Your terrified screams are inaudible drowned In the spiral ahead and consumed in the shape

The spiraling shape will make you go insane (Everyone wants to see that groovy thing) But everyone wants to see that groovy thing (Everyone wants to see that thing)

And now that you've tried it, you're back to report That the spiraling shape was a fraud and a fake You didn't enjoy it, you never believed it There won't be a refund, you'll never go back

The spiraling shape will make you go insane (Everyone wants to see that groovy thing) But everyone wants to see that groovy thing (Everyone wants to see that thing)

And nobody knows what it's really like But everyone says it's great And they heard it from the spiral in their eyes (Spiral in their eyes)

Fogging the view, cupping face to the window In darkness you make out a spiraling shape Putting all reason aside you exchange What you got for a thing that's hypnotic and strange

The spiraling shape will make you go insane (Everyone wants to see that groovy thing) But everyone wants to see that groovy thing (Everyone wants to see that thing)

Don't spend the rest of your life wondering (Everyone wants to see that thing)

Don't spend the rest of your life wondering (Everyone wants to see that groovy thing) Don't spend the rest of your life wondering (Everyone wants to see that thing)

PEACOCK

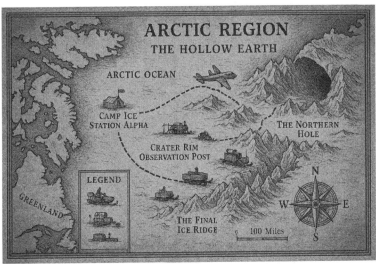

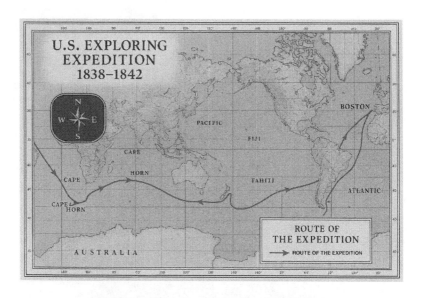

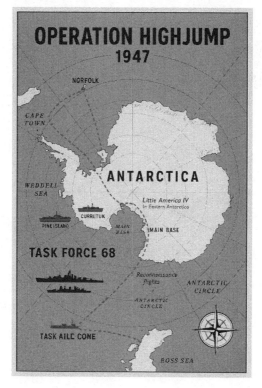

DOUGLAS R4D-5 SKYTRAIN

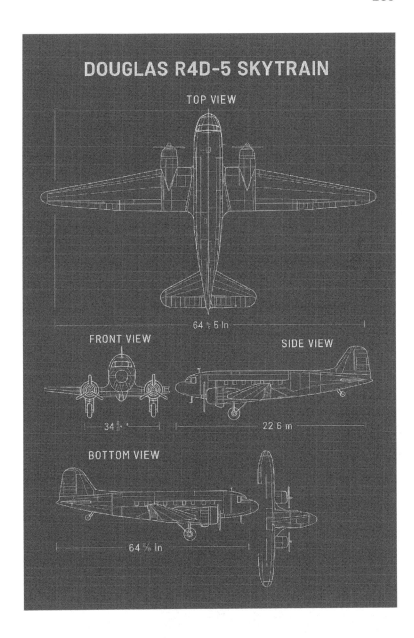

References and Further Reading:

Blavatsky, H. P. 1888. *The Secret Doctrine: The Synthesis of Science, Religion, and Philosophy.* London: Theosophical Publishing Society.

Browne, Sylvia. 2004. *Prophecy: What the Future Holds for You.* New York: Dutton.

Bulwer-Lytton, Edward. 1871. *The Coming Race.* London: George Routledge and Sons.

Byrd, Richard E. 1935. *Discovery: The Story of the Second Byrd Antarctic Expedition.* New York: G.P. Putnam's Sons.

Campbell, Joseph. 1949. *The Hero with a Thousand Faces.* Princeton: Princeton University Press.

Childress, David Hatcher. 1992. *Lost Cities and Ancient Mysteries of South America.* Stelle, IL: Adventures Unlimited Press.

Childress, David Hatcher. 1996. *Hollow Earth: The Greatest Geographical Discovery in History Made by Admiral Richard E. Byrd in the Mysterious Land Beyond the Poles.* Stelle, IL: Adventures Unlimited Press.

Cox, Robert S. 2003. *Body and Soul: A Sympathetic History of American Spiritualism.* Charlottesville: University of Virginia Press.

DeCamp, L. Sprague. 1954. *Lost Continents: The Atlantis Theme in History, Science, and Literature.* New York: Dover Publications.

Emerson, Willis George. 1908. *The Smoky God, or, A Voyage to the Inner World.* Los Angeles: Forbes & Co.

Farrell, Joseph P. 2005. *Reich of the Black Sun: Nazi Secret Weapons and the Cold War Allied Legend.* Kempton, IL: Adventures Unlimited Press.

Flammarion, Camille. 1894. *Popular Astronomy.* London: Chatto & Windus.

Fort, Charles. 1919. *The Book of the Damned.* New York: Boni and Liveright.

Godwin, Joscelyn. 1993. *Arktos: The Polar Myth in Science, Symbolism, and Nazi Survival.* Kempton, IL: Adventures Unlimited Press.

Goodrick-Clarke, Nicholas. 2003. *Black Sun: Aryan Cults, Esoteric Nazism, and the Politics of Identity.* New York: NYU Press.

Halley, Edmond. 1692. "An Account of the Cause of the Change of the Variation of the Magnetic Needle." *Philosophical Transactions* 16(179): 563–578.

Harper, Kristine. 2012. *Weather by the Numbers: The Genesis of Modern Meteorology.* Cambridge, MA: MIT Press.

Huxley, Julian. 1957. *New Bottles for New Wine.* London: Chatto & Windus.

Jansen, Olaf. 1908. *The Smoky God* (as told to Willis George Emerson). Los Angeles: Forbes & Co.

Kircher, Athanasius. 1665. *Mundus Subterraneus.* Amsterdam: Joannem Janssonium.

Kolosimo, Peter. 1971. *Not of This World.* New York: University Books.

Lovecraft, H. P. 1936. *At the Mountains of Madness.* New York: Astounding Stories.

MacDougall, Walter. 1999. *The Oldest Trail: A History of the Maine Forest and Logging Museum.* Orono, ME: University of Maine Press.

MacGregor, Jon. 2017. *Resonant Earth: Sound and the Shaping of Meaning.* London: Resonance Press.

McKenna, Terence. 1992. *Food of the Gods: The Search for the Original Tree of Knowledge.* New York: Bantam.

Mitchell, John. 1983. *The Earth Spirit: Its Ways, Shrines, and Mysteries.* London: Thames & Hudson.

Rucker, Rudy. 1990. *The Hollow Earth: The Narrative of Mason Algiers Reynolds of Virginia.* New York: Arbor House.

Symmes, John Cleves Jr. 1820. *Symmes's Theory of Concentric Spheres: Demonstrating That the Earth Is Hollow, Habitable Within, and Widely Open About the Poles.* Cincinnati: Morgan, Lodge & Fisher.

Verne, Jules. 1864. *Journey to the Center of the Earth.* Leipzig: Pierre-Jules Hetzel.

Wilkes, Charles. 1845. *Narrative of the United States Exploring Expedition.* Philadelphia: Lea & Blanchard.

Zundel, Ernst. 1975. *UFOs: Nazi Secret Weapon?* Toronto: Samisdat Publishers.

8.

About the Author:

Scott Neitlich is a writer, historian, and lifelong explorer of forgotten stories. In addition to his published work, he also runs the highly popular YouTube channel *Spector Creative* offering insights into pop culture, history and media.

He holds an BA from UCSB and an MBA from UNCG.
He lives in Greensboro, North Carolina with his wife, daughter and 10,000 books.

Also available:

Made in the USA
Columbia, SC
26 May 2025